Quick & Easy

SCRAPBOOK PAGES

100 Scrapbook pages you can make in one hour or less

MEMORY MAKERS BOOKS

Executive Editor Kerry Arquette **Founder** Michele Gerbrandt

Editor Shannon Hurd

Art Director Andrea Zocchi

Designer Nick Nyffeler

Craft Editor Jodi Amidei

Idea Editor Janetta Wieneke

Photography Ken Trujillo

Contributing Photographers Marc Creedon, Tara Cruz, Christina Dooley, Brenda Martinez

Contributing Writers Kelly Angard, Torrey Miller, Margaret Radford, Tiffany Spaulding

Editorial Support MaryJo Reiger, Dena Twinem

Special thanks to the editors of *Memory Makers* magazine

Quick & Easy Scrapbook Pages
Copyright © 2003 Memory Makers Books
All rights reserved.

Published by Memory Makers Books, an imprint of F&W Publications, Inc.
12365 Huron Street, Suite 500, Denver, CO 80234 Phone 1-800-254-9124

Library of Congress Cataloging-in-Publication Data

Quick & easy scrapbook pages : 100 scrapbook pages you can make in one hour or less.
    p.cm.
Includes bibliographical references and index.
  ISBN 1-892127-20-2
  1. Photograph albums. 2. Photographs--Conservation and restoration.
3. Scrapbooks. I. Title: Quick and easy scrapbook pages.
  TR465.Q58 2003
  745.593--dc21

                    2003042143

Distributed to trade and art markets by F&W Publications, Inc.
4700 East Galbraith Road, Cincinnati, OH 45236 Phone 1-800-289-0963

First Edition, Printed and bound in the United States of America

07 06 05 04 03 7 6 5 4 3

ISBN 1-892127-20-2

Memory Makers Books is the home of *Memory Makers*, the scrapbook magazine dedicated to educating and inspiring scrapbookers. To subscribe, or for more information, call 1-800-366-6465. Visit us on the Internet at www.memorymakersmagazine.com

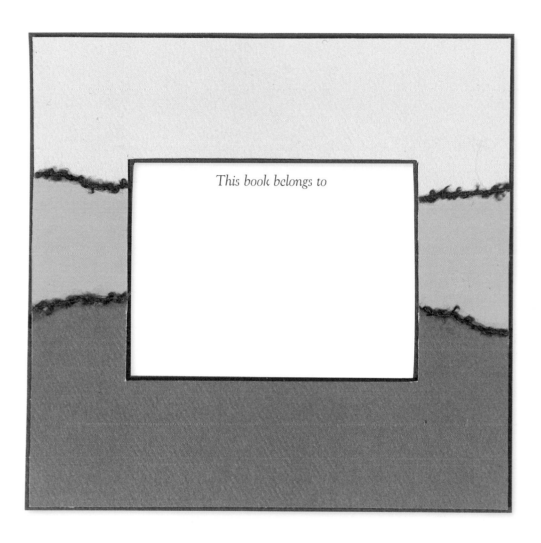

This book belongs to

We dedicate this book to all of our *Memory Makers* readers
who set aside time in their busy lives to scrapbook.

TABLE OF CONTENTS

7 • Introduction

8 • Getting Started
Setting up your scrapbook workspace: ideas for sorting photos and memorabilia; photo-safe storage options; top timesaving tools; a supply shopping checklist.

14 • Layout & Design
Learning how to effectively arrange photos, journaling and embellishments on your page: eleven diverse, ready-to-use design templates; readers' tips for finding time to scrapbook plus an entire section on color psychology. Discover how to choose colors that best support your page's mood and theme!

32 • Backgrounds
Learning to create eye-catching scrapbook page back-grounds: pre-made products; torn paper; color blocking, paper weaving, stamping and other techniques.

48 • Titles, Borders & Mats
Discovering methods for making fast and fun titles, borders and mats: title tags; titles from around-the-house supplies; embellishing stencil titles, sticker titles; punch, sticker, photo and color-blocked borders; embellished mats and more.

Pg 17

Pg 39

Pg 69

74 • Embellishments
Dressing up your scrapbook pages: pre-made products; paper tearing; punches and die cuts; stickers; chalking; stamping; fibers; wire; tags; beads and other embellishments.

98 • Journaling
Setting the words down on the page: innovative ways to incorporate journaling in your scrapbook page designs; cool quotes; interview techniques and questions; power word list and more tips to help you make the most of your time.

114 • Gallery
More beautiful quick and easy scrapbook pages for inspiration.

123 • Glossary

124 • Credits, Sources and Index

Pg 62

Pg 102

Pg 80

DANIEL

While traveling in Alaska in the summer of 2002, we found stuffed animal totems outside of many of the stores. Every time we would see one we stopped to take a picture of Daniel with the animal. We were amazed at how many of them we saw and how much fun it was finding them.

Introduction

Soccer practice. Homework. Meetings. Birthday parties. We are always being pulled in a dozen directions. It's no different at my house, where we're constantly on the go between school, work, home and church. Most days, I am fortunate if I get a peaceful moment, much less five or six uninterrupted hours to scrapbook!

Fortunately, there are ways to work around even the busiest of schedules so you won't have to compromise the hobby that you love. Inside our book, *Quick & Easy Scrapbook Pages*, you'll find numerous examples of attractive, easy-to-assemble layouts that most people can create in an hour or less. You'll also discover dozens of ways to simplify your favorite "complex" scrapbooking techniques, including creating your own backgrounds and unique title, border and mat treatments, as well as dozens of fun and fast ways to add embellishments.

For additional inspiration, we have also included a variety of staff and reader time- and money-saving tips, as well as a sampling of ready-to-use page-design templates, inspirational quotes and a quick tutorial on color-mood psychology. Use any of these techniques to help spice up the content of your pages!

The secret to creating gorgeous scrapbook pages is learning to make the most of the time you have—and not worrying about the time you don't. Complex-looking pages can actually be very easy to make, provided you have supplies on hand, an idea in mind and the enthusiasm to create.

Allow us to show you how!

Michele

Michele Gerbrandt
Founder of *Memory Makers* magazine

Getting Started

All of the scrapbook pages in this book are indeed quick and easy to create. You can make the process even smoother by investing time in preplanning and organization. Begin by setting up a workspace on which you can spread out your photos and memorabilia. The workspace should be out of the direct sunlight. Then sort your photos and memorabilia in a way which will make them easily accessible when you sit down to scrapbook. There are two recognized methods for sorting your materials.

Sorting Photos Chronologically

Gather all of your photographs into one pile. If the photos are still in their original envelopes with the negatives, transfer them to photo-safe envelopes.

- Label the contents of each envelope, or label the dividers in the photo-safe boxes. Include a "best-guess" date as to when the pictures were taken. If there is related memorabilia or journaling you want to include later, note it with a star next to the date.

- Sort the envelopes by date, assigning each envelope a number that will assist you in filing them in consecutive order. Place them in the box. Now, attack the memorabilia: Divide into categories such as *tickets*, *journals*, or *brochures*. Place the items in a labeled and dated memorabilia box.

Sorting Photos By Theme

(Best for wedding, vacation or holiday albums)

Collect all photos and memorabilia. On sticky notes, write down the categories pertinent to your current project. For example, if you are working on a travel album, you
may wish to sort the photos into groups such as *making plans*, *site-seeing* and *adventures*.

- Sort your photos by category into piles near the appropriate sticky notes.

- Re-sort the photos in each pile so they fall in logical order. This is, most often,
  the sequence in which you hope to place the photos in your album.

- Place the sorted piles in labeled, photo-safe envelopes and acid-free boxes,
  storing them until you are ready to scrapbook.

Tools

Like all hobbyists, scrapbookers must invest in a certain number of basics tools in order to create albums. While you're likely to find some tools, such as scissors, tweezers and a straightedge ruler, already reside in your utility drawer, there are others you will have to purchase.

Album, pages and page protectors

Albums come in four styles: three-ring binder, spiral, post or strap bound. The most popular and readily available sizes are 12 x 12" and 8½ x 11". Sturdy, well-constructed, expandable albums are the best and most durable choices, however all albums should be archival-quality environments for your photos and memorabilia. Page protectors, transparent sleeves that cover and protect scrapbook pages, should be made of nonreactive, PVC-free plastic.

Pigment pens and markers

All scrapbook journaling should be done with pigment ink which is lightfast, fade-resistant, waterproof and colorfast. Pigment pens are available in an array of colors and tip widths which make journaling or embellishing easy and fun.

Adhesives

There are a wide range of glues and tapes available that make scrapbooking neat and precise. Adhesives include tape runners, photo mounting squares, glue pens, bottled glue, photo tape and glue dots.

Solid and patterned papers

Paper is used for page backgrounds, mats, frames and embellishments. Scrapbook paper, sold in single sheets, packets and booklets, comes in hundreds of colors and patterns. All should be pH neutral (acid-free) and lignin-free. Many varieties are also buffered.

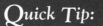

> **Quick Tip:** Clean ink and adhesive residue off of tools and repair tools before storing in a dry, dust-free place. Store all tools and supplies out of the sun. Albums should be stored in an upright position, however paper should be stored flat. Store die cuts and stickers within page protectors inside of binders.

Top Timesaving Tools

Beyond the basics, you may wish to invest in these timesaving tools. They are straight-forward, fun to use and will help you make the very most of your scrapbooking time.

Nested Templates

Easy to store, easy to pack, easy to use. What more could you ask for? These popular "nested" templates quickly create the perfect shapes and sizes for multiple layers of photo mats. Talk about a timesaver!

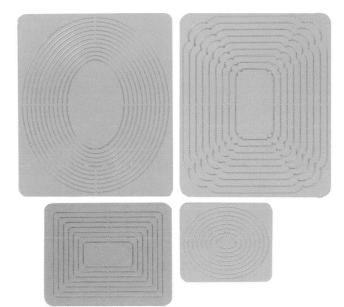

Adhesive Remover

Correct a mistake without sacrificing entire sheets of paper. With a little bit of un-du, an incorrectly placed sticker or other embellishment comes right off your page. The page dries in just minutes with no evidence of the embellishment.

Computer

Of all the scrapbooking tools out there, this baby offers the most bang for your buck. In addition to providing easy access to inspirational quotes and scrapbooking Web sites, many software programs now exist to help you create attractive, unique page embellishments and fonts! Added bonus: Journaling might seem less intimidating with the help of spelling and grammar check!

The Xyron Machine

When applying adhesive to a variety of items, the Xyron machine is in a class by itself. The big advantage Xyron offers over regular adhesives is that it covers 100 percent of the sticking surface when you run items through the machine. This ensures that whatever you wish to make sticky will lie flat on your page and have less chance of catching on a page protector or ripping off the page.

Corner Rounders

Corner rounders give photos a "finished" look instantly. A corner rounder is a good option for anyone who wants to keep it simple.

Top-Loading Page Protectors

These protectors allow you to design your pages on background paper, then simply drop them into the page protectors. They also make it easy to rearrange your album pages without removing the protectors from the binding. Another creative use: Keep a few in your scrapbook bag for storing photos and supplies you plan to use later.

Clear Grid Ruler

This favorite quick and easy tool allows you to measure the width of a mat or border as small as $\frac{1}{16}$". The rulers are available in the quilting section of your local fabric store or in office supply stores. They are relatively inexpensive ($8 to $13) and come in a variety of sizes, but the 12 x 2" size seems the best fit for scrapbooking.

Personal Paper Trimmer

This compact tool makes a quick and easy accessory to any scrapbook project. Cropping photos, trimming mats or cutting thin paper strips takes no time at all with a trimmer. Compact enough to slip into a cropping tote, most personal paper trimmers come with several extra blades that are easy to change.

Supplies shopping checklist

Cut down the time you spend shopping for scrapbook supplies by determining exactly what you need to purchase before ever leaving the house. Photocopy this checklist and use it to preplan in order to make your shopping trip most efficient.

Organizational Supplies

- [ ] Photo box(es)
- [ ] Negative sleeves
- [ ] Photo envelopes
- [ ] Self-stick notes
- [ ] Memorabilia keepers
- [ ] Storage containers

ALBUM TYPES
- [ ] Strap
- [ ] Post bound
- [ ] Spiral
- [ ] 3-ring binder
- [ ] Mini
- [ ] Other

_____
_____

Preferred brand(s)

_____
_____

ALBUM SIZES
- [ ] 4 x 6"
- [ ] 5 x 7"
- [ ] 8½ x 11"
- [ ] 12 x 12"
- [ ] 12 x 15"
- [ ] Other

_____
_____

Preferred brand(s)

_____
_____

ALBUM FILLER PAGES
- [ ] 4 x 6"
- [ ] 5 x 7"
- [ ] 8½ x 11"
- [ ] 12 x 12"
- [ ] 12 x 15"
- [ ] Other

_____
_____

Preferred brand(s)

_____
_____

ALBUM PAGE PROTECTORS
- [ ] 4 x 6"
- [ ] 5 x 7"
- [ ] 8½ x 11"
- [ ] 12 x 12"
- [ ] 12 x 15"

_____
_____

Preferred brand(s)

_____
_____

ARCHIVAL QUALITY ADHESIVES
- [ ] Photo splits
- [ ] Double-sided photo tape
- [ ] Tape roller
- [ ] Liquid glue pen
- [ ] Glue stick
- [ ] Bottled glue
- [ ] Self-adhesive foam spacers
- [ ] Adhesive application machine
- [ ] Adhesive application machine cartridge
- [ ] Adhesive remover
- [ ] Other

_____
_____

Preferred brand(s)

_____
_____

SCISSORS & CUTTERS
- [ ] Small scissors
- [ ] Regular scissors
- [ ] Decorative scissors
- [ ] Paper trimmer
- [ ] Shape cropper(s)
- [ ] Craft knife

PENCILS, PENS, MARKERS
- [ ] Pigment pen(s)
- [ ] Photo-safe pencil
- [ ] Vanishing ink pen

RULERS & TEMPLATES
- [ ] Metal straightedge ruler
- [ ] Grid ruler
- [ ] Decorative ruler(s)
- [ ] Journaling template(s)
- [ ] Shape template(s)
- [ ] Letter template(s)
- [ ] Nested template(s)

ACID- AND LIGNIN-FREE PAPER
- [ ] Red
- [ ] Orange
- [ ] Yellow
- [ ] Brown
- [ ] Green
- [ ] Blue
- [ ] Purple
- [ ] Pink
- [ ] Black
- [ ] White
- [ ] Patterns

_____

- [ ] Themes

_____
_____

- [ ] Vellum color(s)

_____
_____

- [ ] Mulberry color(s)

_____
_____

- [ ] Specialty paper(s)

_____
_____

- [ ] Other

Preferred brand(s)

_____
_____

STICKERS
Themes or types

_____
_____
_____
_____
_____

DIE CUTS
Themes or types

_____
_____
_____
_____

PUNCHES
- [ ] Corner rounder
- [ ] Hand punch(es)
- [ ] Border(s)
- [ ] Decorative corner(s)
- [ ] Photo mounting
- [ ] Shape(s)

- [ ] Tweezers
- [ ] Wax paper
- [ ] Aluminum foil

RUBBER STAMPS
Themes or types

_____
_____
_____
_____
_____

- [ ] Ink pad(s)
- [ ] Embossing powder(s)
- [ ] Stamp cleaner

Summer gives us so much —
strength, light, food. No car
trips on icy roads to gather
wilted produce imported from
far away, from parts of the
world where warmth lingers.
Instead, you can pick ripe
fruit from your own trees and
savor the taste of juicy fruit,
still warm from the sun.
Lauren gathered bushels of ripe
pears this year to make into
chutney. When we open them
this winter, I hope we'll be
able to taste the freshness, the
warmth and the joy that only
summer can give us. We can
savor the taste and dream of
those lazy days of summer.

Summer Fruits

Chapter 1
Layout & Design

Of those elements that contribute to the overall look of a complete scrapbook page, layout and design are among the most important. You could have the most powerful photographs, journaling and embellishments in the world, but if they are misplaced or if your color selection is off base, your page's "wow" factor falls flat.

Keep in mind that each scrapbooker has her own unique method for determining page layout. Some scrapbookers shuffle and rearrange pieces hundreds of times before finally stumbling upon a look they like. Others begin with a very specific concept in mind, then quickly move forward to bring it to fruition.

The most helpful theory to keep in mind when designing quick and easy scrapbook pages is that less is often more. Cluttering pages with extraneous embellishments or trying to fit too many photos and other elements on a page not only takes time, but muddies the final product.

So think sleek, lean and clean as you let the fun begin!

Templates

There are many ways to arrange your photos and memorabilia on a scrapbook page. You may keep everything in the center, scatter it across the border, or create a zig-zag pattern. While the choice is yours, you can use these pre-made page templates for additional inspiration.

We are so in love with summer. How is it the longest days of the year go by so quickly?! This is Annie's first visit to Lake Michigan and her first lake sunset. When I saw Annie running in and out of the water, heard her giggles and squeals of delight echoing over the waves, watched Mike scoop her up in his arms proudly...I knew this was

better than any summer dream I could ever have. This is real. This is my life. Giggles, excitement, wonderment every day — winter, spring, summer, and fall — We are in love with them all as long as we have each other.

Summer Dreamin'

Summer Dreamin'

ENLARGE PHOTO FOR DRAMATIC PRESENCE

Cherri captures the beauty of an enchanting summer evening by using an enlarged photo to serve as the focal point of her page. Mount large photo on black background paper. Mat smaller photos on extra copy of sunset photo to complement colors in large photo. Print title and text on transparency; mount on large photo.

Cherri Weir, Lapeer, Michigan

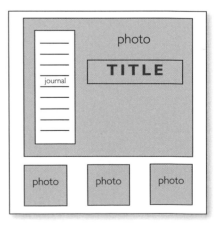

Windswept

DRESS UP SIMPLE LAYOUT WITH FIBER

A succession of three enlarged, candid photos stands out on Mary Anne's simple, impactful layout. Print journaling and title on patterned paper (Faux Memories); layer over solid paper, leaving ¼" border. Mat all three photos on solid colored paper; tear top and bottom of matting before mounting on page. Embellish with fibers (Memory Crafts) wrapped along bottom of page.

Mary Anne Walters, Monk Sherborne, UK

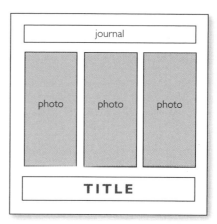

Quick Tip: While a large photo provides a dramatic focal point for your spread, you can achieve the same effect by double matting a slightly smaller photo such as a 5 x 7".

Mother

PAPER TEAR BORDERS AND PHOTO MATS

Christina adds interest to simple black-and-white photos with tearing and photo mats. Tear solid and patterned papers (Mustard Moon); layer on page to create side borders. Mount large photo. Crop rectangles from solid paper to layer behind smaller photos; tear one side. Add torn paper strip; embellish with flowers (Emagination Crafts, EK Success) punched from solid and vellum papers. Glue seed beads (Crafts Etc.) to center of flowers. Print text on vellum; tear edges and mat on solid paper with eyelets (Doodlebug Design). Print balance of title on solid paper; silhouette-cut letters with a craft knife.

Christina Gibson, Jonesboro, Arkansas

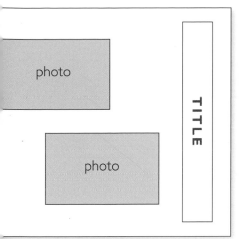

TITLE

a Mother

When do you scrapbook?

"I'm a stay-at-home mother of two children—an almost 4-year-old boy and a 9-month-old girl. While my daughter is napping, I try and get my son excited about working on our scrapbooks together. He has a table just his size next to my work station, along with his own special bin of supplies. I can usually get a couple of pages done while he works on his own book. I think he enjoys scrapbooking almost as much as I do!"

Diane Elderbroom, Wylie, Texas

"For me it's not a matter of finding time to scrapbook—I make the time, because it's important to me that my children understand their backgrounds. Even though I have a scrapbook room, I lay my 'in progress' pages on the kitchen counter until they're complete. This way I can work on them throughout the day while tending to my family's needs. I found once I started this routine, I was getting at least a page a day done."

Chrystal Wilson, Alexandria, Virginia

"My mom and I commit one evening a week to scrapbooking together, deemed Arts and Crafts Night. After enjoying a nice family dinner and tucking the kids into bed, we meet at the craft table for serious business, where prizes are awarded and winning pages are displayed. Sometimes, I invite another friend to join us. The time together has strengthened our relationship, is therapeutic, and just plain fun."

Lori Haas, Battle Ground, Washington

"I organize layouts into smaller projects, sorting and cropping my photos first, then planning bags with photos and embellishments as needed. I save large layouts for cropping parties. It's the 1-2 page layouts - life's tidbits - that I scrapbook at my small table in the family room, working around family activities. Scrapbooking is like my diary I never got started. It's briefly making sense of the day."

Lynne Moore, Henderson, Nevada

Cousins Photo Shoot

FEATURE A MULTI PHOTO LAYOUT

Beth captures the fun of a homemade photo shoot with a simple, balanced layout. Crop photos; arrange and adhere to page. Print journaling on vellum; tear and chalk edges. Use a template to create "Cousins" title. Punch flowers (Colorbök) and mini trees (McGill). Detail flowers and "Cousins" with metallic rub-ons (Craf-T) and chalk; mount on vellum journaling block. Cut heads off pins and adhere to flower centers. Print second journaling block directly on photo scrap.

Beth Rogers, Mesa, Arizona

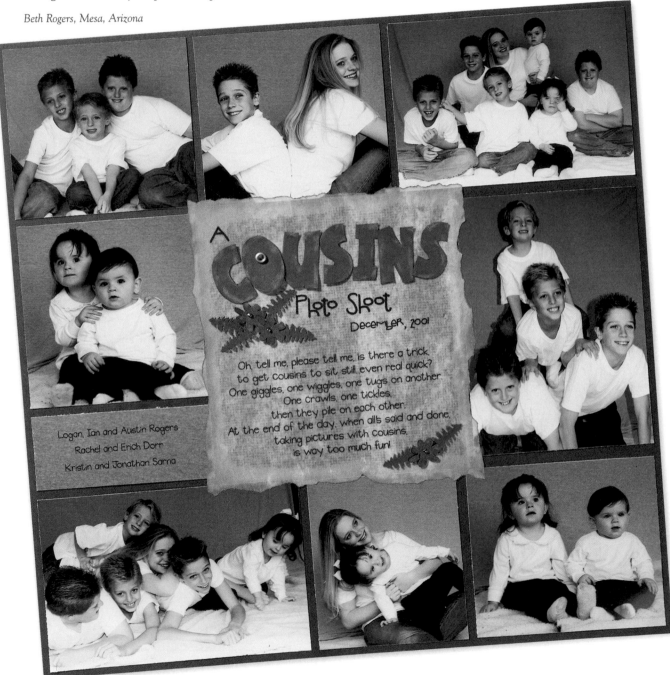

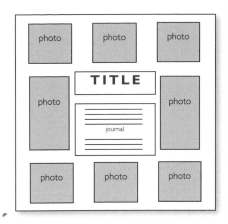

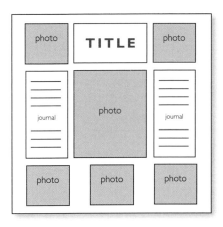

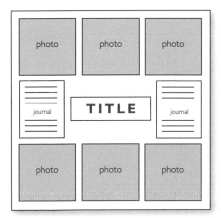

Variations

Use these templates to create variations of the Multi Photo Layout page (on left). All layouts will allow you to showcase numerous photos on a single page and still leave room for title and journaling.

How do you find time to scrapbook?

"Many of us at work are really into scrapbooking, so we have set up a table dedicated to working on our books. At lunch time (which could be at weird times of the day for some of us), we sit around working on our books. The best part is that we share a lot of our supplies, making things a little more fun, interesting and certainly cheaper!"

Molly Vincent, Ellicott City, Maryland

"Whenever we go on a 3-hour trip to Wisconsin to see family and friends, I trace letters on cardstock before we leave, cut them out and mat them for whatever title or titles I'm working on. My husband usually drives and It's hard for me to sit still for three hours anyway, so it makes the time go by faster. Next thing I know, we are there!"

Sheila Boehmert, Island Lake, Illinois

"Whenever my husband and I travel for work, I bring along a small file of pictures I want to work on next, then visit the local store and browse for new ideas and products I haven't seen at home. I also carry a 12 x 12" paper sleeve and resealable plastic bags to store the paraphernalia (such as travel brochures) I collect along the way. When I get home, I can place everything in one folder to enable me to get going quickly when I scrap."

Stephanie Hackney, Carlsbad, California

"One Friday each month, my girlfriends and I get together for some scrapbooking 'girl time.' Meeting in each others' homes and sharing lunches enables us more time to scrap. Sharing tools and ideas, along with lots of laughter, inspires both creative ideas and deepens our close friendship. Each time we scrap together is a blessing from God."

Pam Willis, Aiken, South Carolina

The thing I find easiest is to spend one night cropping pictures for several hours, usually at a workshop away from home. I also lay out my pages with sticker ideas and Post it notes. Then, on nights when I'm really tired, I sit in front of the TV after the kids have gone to bed and simply attach photos to the pages. This way, I use one night to be creative, and the other to relax and just stick things down."

Rachelle St. Phard, East Windsor, New Jersey

Daydream

BALANCE PAGE WITH LARGE AND SMALL PHOTOS

Sandra offsets an enlarged photo of her daughter on the beach with two smaller snapshots nestled into the lower left-hand corner of the page. Print title and poem on background paper. Triple-mat large photo, first on mesh paper, then on patterned (source unknown) and solid papers. Layer small cropped photos over mesh paper and solid paper strip; embellish with seashells (U.S. Shell, Inc.).

Sandra Stephens, Eden Prairie, Minnesota

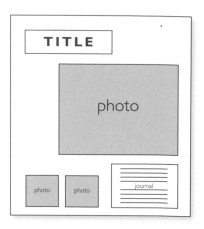

On cool Autumn days
And snowy winter days
Daydream of the time,
The lazy days of summer,
Filled with sunshine and warmth
And remember
The salty smell of the sea
Splashing in the warm water
The sand running through your fingers
And the glow of the beautiful sunsets

Nothing Is Impossible

ILLUSTRATE PHOTO WITH TITLE QUOTE

A charming photo stands alone on Janice's simple and appealing layout. Print title quote on background paper; punch heart (EKSuccess) and mount. Print journaling onto solid-colored cardstock; cut paper strip and mount on page. Mat photo and mount.

Janice Carson, Hamilton, ON, Canada

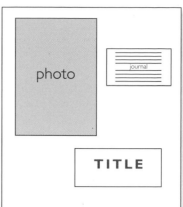

Jonathan is trying to climb an old plough at the Logging Museum in Algonquin Park. He is a very determined little boy. July, 2002

Nothing is impossible to a willing heart. ♥

The Calm
PAPER-TEAR PATTERNED PAPER BACKGROUND

Oksanna allows one photo to fill a two-page spread by extending gray matting onto the opposite page. Print part of title and journaling on background paper and photo mat. Diagonally tear patterned paper (Design Originals); mount at upper left and lower right hand corners of background paper. Triple-mat photo; use mat with journaling as the third photo mat. Slice gray paper strip with partial title for opposite page; tuck under torn patterned paper. Cut large title word from template (C-Thru Ruler). Adhere seashell stickers (Provo Craft) to title and photo mats. Stamp seashell design (Duncan); silhouette-cut and mount on page.

Oksanna Pope, Los Gatos, California

Silly
ADD DETAILS TO A SIMPLE LAYOUT

Andrea captures her daughter's smile on a simple layout dressed up with charming details. Mat embossed paper (Jennifer Collection) and one photo; mount both photos on page. Print title and journaling on vellum; cut to size and add chalk highlights. Attach eyelets (Impress Rubber Stamps) to title and text blocks. Tie fiber and mount sunglasses button (Jesse James). Attach fiber (source unknown) across middle of page, securing behind handmade paper. Lightly snip edges of fiber to achieve frayed look.

Andrea Hautala, Olympia, Washington

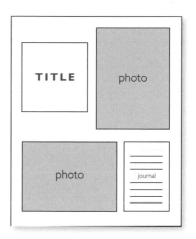

Color Selection

One of the first steps in designing a scrapbook page is to decide upon the color palette. These are the shades and hues you will use for background papers, mats, frames and embellishments. You can select colors for your pages in a number of ways.

Pull color from your photos

While you may be tempted to choose a color that dominates your photos, this may cause your photos to blend with their background, rather than pop off the page. Instead, select a secondary color from your pictures and use the primary color sparingly. Refuse to allow your color choices to be dictated by the theme of your page, if this means that colors and photos will clash. For example, if your daughter's Christmas dress is orange, you may wish to shy away from traditional red and green holiday layouts.

Color Psychology 101

Personality characteristics most commonly associated with colors:

Red—power, intensity, passion, competition, sexuality

Orange—enthusiasm, vibrancy, flamboyance

Yellow—optimism, happiness, idealism, energy, imagination

Green—loyalty, intelligence, fertility, healing, ecology

Blue—peace, tranquility, harmony, trust, confidence

Purple—mystery, royalty, spirituality, creativity, unconventional

Pink—tender, feminine, romantic, affectionate, dainty

Gray—sadness, security, reliability, routine, lifeless

Brown—stability, simplicity, comfort, practicality, conservatism

Black—mournful, heavy, depressing, sophisticated, mysterious

White—cleanliness, purity, youth, simplicity, innocence

A Color Wheel

A color wheel is the perfect tool to help you find a variety of color combinations to complement or to contrast with the colors in your photos. A color wheel is easy to use. Point to your chosen color on the color wheel and arrows point you in the direction of great accent colors. Additional instructions included with the wheel will help you further utilize it. Learning to combine colors will bring new excitement to your layouts.

Hangin' With Goofy

COLOR SCHEME DEFINES PAGE

The golden color of Goofy's shirt as well as the jewel hues from the background curtain and children's clothes are perfect choices for this fun and simple design. The clean white background paper provides a neutral base for the vibrant page accents.

Torrey Miller, Westminster, Colorado

Color and Emotion

Studies show that exposure to certain colors elicits different emotions and behaviors in people by activating specific brain pathways, causing them to release particular neurochemicals. For example, yellow stimulates appetite while pink can accelerate healing. But how can this theory benefit your scrapbook pages? Use the chart below to help select the perfect colors to accompany your page's mood.

Sporty Colors like bright red, blue, yellow and green, are sharp, witty and unique. Looking at them, you can almost feel the energy taking fire within. Use them to scrapbook athletic events, such as football games, baseball practices or cheerleading tryouts. Or add a dash of excitement and sparkle to family activities, like trips to the amusement park, circus or zoo. They may be perfect to convey intense emotion.

Earthy Tones such as tan, chestnut brown, olive green and deep burgundy evoke a strong sense of inner peace, tranquility and well-being. They remind us of meaningful conversations with family and friends and can be used to help dispel loneliness. A great choice for scrapbooking nature-oriented activities such as hiking, camping, raking leaves or lazy Sunday afternoon strolls in the park.

Tropical Colors like bubble gum pink, teal, bright yellow and lime green are fun, exciting, whimsical hues. They charge the body with a playful sense of energy and vitality, instilling a rich sense of joyful freedom. Use these colors to scrapbook childhood activities such as birthday parties, swim meets and parades. Or, choose holiday-oriented themes, like dyeing Easter eggs.

Jewel Colors such as copper, gold, royal blue and deep purple command respect without being overbearing. They help convey the message that an individual is intelligent, well-traveled and has something important to say. The best activities to scrapbook with these "jems" are accomplishments—think graduations, promotions or special honors and awards.

Tranquil Colors such as slate blue, wintergreen and buttercup inspire feelings of refreshment and rejuvenation within your soul. By seeping into your conscience and silencing your innermost fears, they evoke those peaceful feelings experienced when reading, writing, sleeping in or cuddling with your significant other in front of the fireplace.

Dark Colors like navy blue, forest green and brick red are solemn, more sophisticated tones. Typically associated with maturity, stability and seriousness, use these hues to pay tribute to the elders in your life. A Father's Day page would be great!

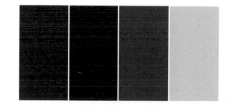

Ethnic Colors like dandelion yellow, mahogany and plum are oozing with mystery and spice. They are perfect for scrapbooking the unfamiliar—maybe a first-time vacation to a far-away land, or a Saturday night salsa date with that hot, handsome stranger.

Cool Colors such as sky blue and sage green provide a calming ambiance by sweeping feelings of relaxation, focus and meditation throughout your body. A wonderful seasonal hue, cool colors are most commonly associated with winter, but can also convey feelings of peaceful summer afternoons as seen on "Simplicity" (page 31).

Country Tones like dusty red and frosted blue are most commonly associated with feelings of coziness, homeliness, and security—think momma's cute little white-picket-fenced house. The events you choose to scrapbook using these tones may vary. Perhaps a homemade chili dinner served around a warm fire?

Victorian Colors such as rusty gold and royal velvet conjure up images that are old-fashioned, awe-inspiring and even somewhat intimidating. Many people choose to use these colors on their heritage pages. Nothing says authentic 19th century better than the antique velvet shades of your great-grandmother's favorite dress!

Romantic Hues including soft pastels such as apricot, periwinkle and buttercup, have an interesting ability to halt the body's desire to stay angry. Exuding femininity and innocence, they are perfect for capturing life's precious, tender events like the birth of a baby, a spring wedding, Easter Sunday and any "girl themed" pages.

Chic Hues such as blue-gray, black and burnt sienna exude elegance, sophistication and class. Most commonly associated with intelligence, these colors are perfect for scrapbooking professional events like first days on the job, work presentations and public speaking endeavors or anything that screams "businesswoman in suit!"

Fever

USE MONOCHROMATIC COLOR SCHEME
TO ENHANCE LAYOUT THEME

Dee uses vibrant, lively colors to reflect her son's physical discomfort over a 102-degree fever. Tear edges of solid paper, chalking around torn edges. Mount on background paper; tear vellum and patterned paper (Paper Adventures) strips; layer at top and bottom of page. Cut title using template (Scrap Pagerz) and patterned paper; mat on solid paper and silhouette. Layer on vellum strip over fibers. Mat photos on torn patterned and solid papers. Print text on vellum; tear edges and mount. Embellish bottom of page with fibers, tag (Avery) and brads (American Tag Company).

Dee Gallimore-Perry, Griswold, Connecticut

Simplicity

SET THE TONE WITH COOL COLORS

Jodi's choice of a cool color palette reflects the calm and carefree mood of her seaside photos. Build a color-blocked background by cutting rectangles in shades of green and plum; layer on page as shown. Mount photos on page. Trace type font lettering onto vellum; tear around edges and mount. Adhere starfish (Crafts, Etc.).

Jodi Amidei, Memory Makers
Photos, Kimberly Wall, Palm City, Florida

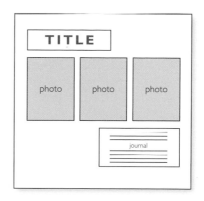

Sand

Sand

sand

no one can tell me
nobody knows
where the wind comes from
where the wind goes

it's flying from somewhere
as fast as it can
it swirls, and twirls
and makes dunes in the sand

when she got home
she had sand in her hair
in her eyes, and her ears
sand everywhere

and to this day
when a strong west wind blows
haley is found with
sand in her toes

adapted from poetry written
by A.A. Milne

Chapter 2
Backgrounds

One of the easiest ways to create an attractive scrapbook page is to design your own background. In doing so, you're assured of a one-of-a-kind scrapbook design. And you'll buy yourself hours of scrapbooking time by eliminating the need to rush about town in search of that perfect piece of paper to match your page theme.

In this chapter you'll find dozens of terrific quick and easy backgrounds that can be made by incorporating commonly used scrapbooking techniques including paper tearing, stamping and color blocking. These ideas can be customized for your page themes, whether it's a spread illustrating the steep granite mountains of Yosemite National Park or a bright, boldly colored page mimicking the cheery lines in a child's sweater.

Whether you're dressing, cooking or constructing album pages, you must begin by creating a basic form. The satin and lace, the icing and candy flowers or the matted and mounted photos will sit prettier on just the right foundation.

Pre-Made Product

Designed with super-easy layout in mind, pre-made backgrounds and page components come in a variety of colors, patterns and themes. Just place your photos, title and journaling.

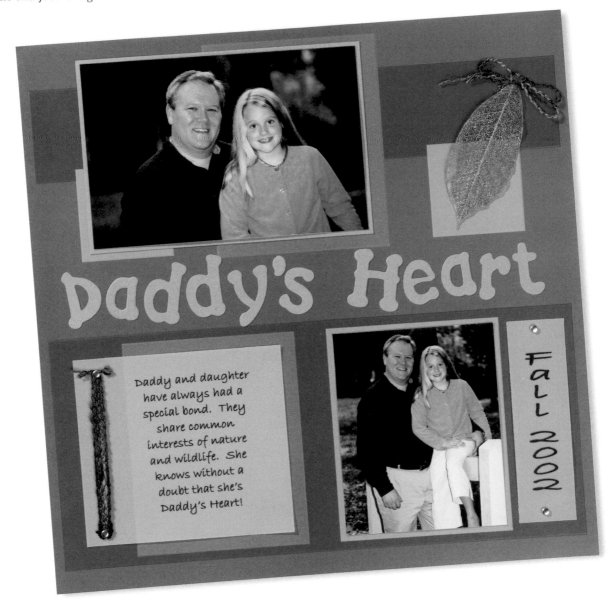

Daddy and daughter have always had a special bond. They share common interests of nature and wildlife. She knows without a doubt that she's Daddy's Heart!

Daddy's Heart

EMBELLISH PREPRINTED PAPER

Valerie adds a personal touch to preprinted and designed background paper with textured embellishments. Mat photos; mount on background paper (All My Memories). Mount die cut letters (Accu Cut) at center of page. Print journaling and photo caption onto vellum; mount on page with small brads (Impress Rubber Stamps). Wrap fibers (On The Surface) around brads. Mount skeleton leaf (Graphic Products Corp.) on page; tie fibers into bow and mount on page.

Valerie Barton, Flowood, Mississippi

Portrait of an Artist

USE COORDINATING PAPERS TO ADD COLOR

Tracy used a coordinating patterned paper set (SEI) to create borders, mat photos and enhance text blocks with lots of color and style. Single, double and triple mat photos on solid and patterned paper. Slice strips of patterned paper; mount on page as a bottom and side border. Print title and text on vellum; mount over patterned paper with eyelets (Doodlebug Design). Adhere sticker letters (Colorbök) on title block.

Tracy Miller, Fallston, Maryland

portrait of
the
ARTiST
at work

Meredith is amazing. She loves to do everything that her big sister does. And she does it well. In these pictures she is engaging in one of her favorite pastimes. She loves to paint and is so intent on the process, although she is not as concerned with the product!

April 2002

Straight Up

TEAR A STAMPED BORDER

Oksanna recreated the solid rock walls she encountered at Yosemite by stamping gray paper with different colors of ink before tearing and mounting on her page. Print title on solid and vellum papers. Mat one photo on vellum; tear on one side. Stamp sand (All Night Media) in various shades of gray and brown to resemble granite. Tear paper and mount at left side of page. Cut first letter of title from template (C-Thru Ruler); mount over torn paper. Layer vellum and photos on right page.

Oksanna Pope, Los Gatos, California

Quick Tip: Tearing paper of all textures and thicknesses offers a decorative edge that softens a page's look. Vary the direction, speed and angle of your tear to achieve surprising and spontaneous results.

Perspectives

ADD FIBER TO PAPER-TORN EDGES

Soft, delicate fibers border paper-torn edges on Jodi's monochromatic page. Follow the instructions below to complete this fun background. Slice window at bottom of page; attach memory keeper (C-Thru Ruler) and trim with fiber. Print journaling onto vellum. Stamp shadow boxes (Hero Arts) and title letters (Plaid Enterprises). Cut to size and layer on page with matted photos.

Jodi Amidei, Memory Makers
Photos, Torrey Miller, Westminster, Colorado

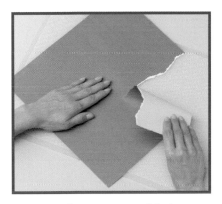

1 Vertically tear piece of darkest green cardstock into a rectangle approximately ⅓ the height of the original page. Tear medium green cardstock the same way.

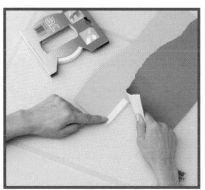

2 Adhere dark green cardstock to medium green cardstock, overlapping slightly.

3 Mount dark and medium green cardstocks on light green cardstock.

4 Using a fine-tipped glue pen, apply glue to torn edges; push fiber into glue. Work in small sections.

Aysha and I

WEAVE A TORN MULBERRY BACKGROUND

Trudy's softly woven mulberry background reflects the tenderness of a mother-daughter moment. Gently tear mulberry paper (PSX, Scrapbook Sally) into strips of various widths, using the method shown below. Loosely weave strips using an under/over technique; mount to white background. Print title and journaling onto vellum; mount on page. Mat photo on paper, leaving room at bottom for embellishing. Adorn title block and photo mat with colored fibers (DMC) and glass pebbles (Magic Scraps).

Trudy Sigurdson
Victoria, BC, Canada

 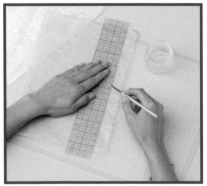 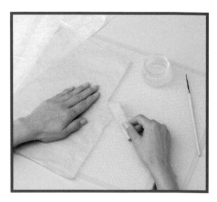

1 Line up grid ruler vertically across edge of mulberry.

2 Dip paintbrush lightly into water and draw line down the edge of the paper, following ruler's edge.

3 Gently tear mulberry along water-lined edge to create frayed look.

Nature's Colors

PAPER TEAR A COLORFUL BACKGROUND

Kelly pulls natures colors from her photos and weaves them into a vibrantly
colored background. Tear approximately ½" paper strips from a variety of
solid-colored papers. Weave together using the under/over technique. Single
and double mat photos. Print partial title and journaling onto vellum, leaving room for balance of title. Cut title letters from template (EK Success)
onto patterned paper (Karen Foster Design); outline with black pen.

Kelly Angard, Highlands Ranch, Colorado

Color Blocking

Creating blocks of color to serve as the background pattern adds dynamic dimension to your pages. Experiment with tried-and-true, as well as less common, color combinations. Don't be afraid to use patterns as well as solids for a truly contemporary effect.

Friends

FRAME PHOTO WITH MUTED COLORS

Holly pieced together a simple color-blocked background of muted colors to frame a favorite childhood photo. Divide page into equal quadrants; cut solid-colored paper to fit quadrants and mount. Mat photo. Print title and photo caption on vellum (Close To My Heart); cut to size and mount.

Holly Van Dyne, Mansfield, Ohio

The Many Faces of Cade
HAND-STITCH PHOTO CAPTIONS

Candice chronicles the many expressions of her baby nephew's face on a patterned paper (Colorbök) that gives the illusion of a color-blocked design. Crop photos all the same size. Print title, journaling and photo captions on vellum (Keeping Memories Alive). Cut to size and hand-stitch onto page with embroidery floss (DMC).

Candice Cruz, Somerville, Massachusetts

Quick Tip: Don't worry about a lack of journaling space on crowded scrapbook pages. Simply print portions of your journaling on vellum. Apply directly over photos, or portions of photos. Your images will shine through and your words will still be conveyed.

Autumn
COLOR BLOCK WITH PATTERNED PAPER

Katie ventured into unknown scrapbooking territory by using Twistel and a color-blocking design for her background. Divide page into three sections; cut coordinating patterned paper (Scrap Ease) into rectangles to fit each section. Mount on solid-colored background paper. Mount eyelets (Emagination Crafts) at each corner. Thread Twistel (Making Memories) through eyelets to frame page. Double mat photo on patterned paper and vellum; mount photo with clear corners. Cut large title letters from template (Scrap Pagerz); mat and silhouette cut. Print balance of title and photo caption onto solid-colored paper. Cut to size and layer under vellum strip.

Katie Swanson, South Milwaukee, Wisconsin

> ## *Quick Tip:*
> Layer a piece of solid 8½ x 11" paper on top of a patterned piece of 12 x 12" cardstock for a quick, eye-catching matting effect (or, leave your background solid and layer patterned paper on top of it).

Freedom
DISTRESS PATTERNED PAPER

Diana uses coordinating papers from the same manufacturer to create quick and easy color-blocked pages. Print title and journaling onto patterned (Provo Craft) and vellum papers. Divide page into quadrants; cut patterned paper to fit sections, as shown in the steps below. Gently sand edges of all paper pieces with fine-grade sandpaper. Mat photo and mount. Layer tag with photo, printed vellum and patterned paper. Gently curl edges of torn patterned paper with finger for a worn look. Add eyelet (Creative Impressions) and stitched star button (Just Another Button Company); tie fiber through eyelet.

Diana Hudson, Bakersfield, California

1 Using grid ruler, determine size of four blocks for background. Background sections may be any size you wish.

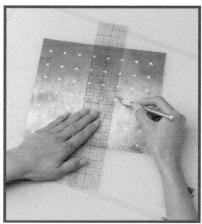

2 Cut out blocks using craft knife or paper trimmer.

3 Mount in sections to background paper using whatever adhesive you desire.

Jeanette Likes

SLICE A STRIPED BACKGROUND

Andrea finds inspiration for her page in her daughter's colorfully striped sweater. Slice strips of colored paper in varying widths; mount side by side on page. Print title, journal list and captions on vellum. Cut to size; mount on page with large eyelets (Impress Rubber Stamps) and clear vellum adhesive. Mount flower embellishments (Hirschberg Schutz & Co.).

Andrea Hautala, Olympia, Washington

Somers Family Reunion

ADD DIMENSION WITH VELLUM LAYERS

Sara layers vellum scraps over torn mulberry to achieve a soft, color-blocked background look. Mount torn mulberry (Bazzill) square onto background. Mount vellum strips in a variety of dimensions over one another as shown. Print title and journaling onto clear vellum (Paper Adventures); cut to size and mount on page.

Sara Perlberg, Milwaukee, Wisconsin

Leia

COLOR BLOCK A MONOCHROMATIC BACKGROUND

Shawn enhanced the natural setting of her photos with an elegant, monochromatic background. Begin by dividing page into quadrants; crop solid-colored paper to size. Mat photo on white paper; adhere decorative leaves (Graphic Products Corp.) at corners and mount over vellum onto page. Mount antique leather strap to page. Cut vellum frame for smaller photo; mount on white paper strip and over leather strap. Print title and text on vellum; layer on background and solid paper strip. Anchor text block in antique clip.

Shawn Baker, Maywood, Missouri

Haley Jo

STAMP SEASONAL COLOR-BLOCKED BACKGROUND

Torrey adds understated impact with seasonal trees stamped on a muted, color-blocked background. Divide page into four sections. Cut rectangles from solid-colored papers to fit sections. Stamp seasonal trees (Hero Arts) using Versa Mark (Tsukineko) creating a watermark effect. Print title onto paper. Mount all rectangles, leaving space between each piece. Mat photo; mount on background. Mount buttons (Making Memories) at photo corners.

Torrey Miller, Westminster, Colorado

Blooms

STAMP A BACKGROUND

Jodi stamped a colorful background using a stipple brush, four colors of ink and a mosaic overlay (DieCuts With A View). Follow the steps below to create this stamped background. Double and triple mat photos. Freehand-write journaling; cut to size, stamp edges and mat. Stamp title letters (Hero Arts); cut to size and mat on two sizes of punched squares (Family Treasures). Stamp flower and leaf design (Hero Arts, DL Designs, Judi Kins); silhouette cut and mount.

Jodi Amidei, Memory Makers

Photos, Michele Gerbrandt

1 Punch out/remove squares in mosaic overlay.

2 Using temporary adhesive, tape down edges of mosaic overlay to white background/cardstock.

3 Lightly touch stipple brush to ink pad and "pounce" over entire mosaic overlay, varying intensity. Repeat with three other ink colors.

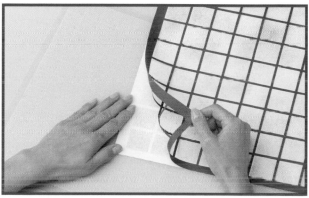

4 Remove mosaic overlay revealing beautifully stamped pattern.

When I was a little girl I used to dream about my prince charming. He would be strong, but also gentle and caring. I always dreamed he would be dark and tall. Most of all, I dreamed of how he would love me and care for me. Now, I'm living that dream. It sounds so corny, but Tom is my prince charming. He is all I could have ever dreamed of, and so much more. What a wonder fairy tale type of love we share.

Tom

Chapter 3
Titles, Borders & Mats

The three basic elements of scrapbooking are photos, journaling and memorabilia. But experienced scrapbookers recognize that those important pieces are better showcased on beautiful pages that include titles, borders and matting.

A title heads a scrapbook page, acts as an important focal point and helps orient the viewer so she can be better prepared to put the pictures and journaling in perspective. Borders and mats bring balance and focus to featured photos. Titles, borders and mats all add an exciting artistic touch to a page.

In this chapter, there are dozens of quick and easy examples of outstanding title, border and mat treatments. Whether dressed up or down, these page ideas are sure to garner attention.

Titles

A strong title is a descriptive headline that sums up the theme of a scrapbook page. It can set the scene and supply basic information. Titles should also be a principal part of a page design. Handmade and pre-made tags are perfect for creative title treatments for a multitude of looks. You may also wish to dress up your titles by stenciling, adding stickers or using around-the-house materials.

Gulf Shores Beach

IMPLEMENT TAGS INTO YOUR TITLE

Beautifully embellished tags enhance Andrea's page and serve as a creative place for photo titles. Tear solid-colored paper at top and bottom; mount over patterned background paper (Colorbök). Mount photos on torn paper; add descriptive words with light gray pen. Print title words; silhouette using craft knife. Embellish tags with fibers (Fibers by the Yard); adhere sticker letter capitals (Me & My Big Ideas/MAMBI) and pen remaining letters.

Andrea Steed, Rochester, Minnesota

Bloom Where You're Planted

PHOTO-EMBELLISHED HANDMADE TAGS

Christie's handmade tags provide a perfect spot for title words and cropped photos.
Single and double mat photos. Print title words on solid-colored paper. Craft handmade
tags around words; embellish with flower eyelets (Stamp Doctor), paper yarn (Making
Memories), cropped photos and pen details. Use die-cut letters (Ellison/Provo Craft) for
large title word; chalk around edges for dimension. Print journaling on vellum; mount
on cardstock, shade with chalk and add paper yarn. Complete page with wire (Artistic
Wire) and bead (Westrim) details.

Christie Scott, Trevor, Wisconsin

Little Man at Work
EMBELLISH WITH REALISTIC MATERIALS

Tina incorporates real building materials into her layout to enhance the construction theme. Cut drywall tape to width of page. Stamp with black ink and set with clear embossing powder. Mat photos; mount on matted background paper. Mount game tiles (Hasbro) as title. Print journaling onto vellum; cut to size. Double mat and mount with small brads (Hyglo/American Pin). Print construction sign from computer (Microsoft Clip Art); cut to size and mount.

Tina Baggott, N. Augusta, South Carolina

Creative Titles With Creative Materials

While there is a plethora of products available for scrapbookers who wish to create outstanding titles, you can find wonderful supplies for embellishing your work right in your own home. Check out your utility drawer, your sewing bin, toy boxes and art areas for bits and pieces that can be turned into works of art.

Kelli Noto, Centennial, Colorado

PLAYTIME

Letter tiles (The Paper Magic Group) linked together set the tone for playful pages. Mount tiles on background. Frame with paper squares cut in a variety of sizes; mount to back of matting as shown.

WILD THING

Add fuzzy texture to titles in the shape of letters with chenille pipe cleaners (Westrim). Bend pipe cleaners into letter shapes; mount on matted background. Adhere animal-print border stickers (Frances Meyers).

FINGER PAINT

Create a realistic title to showcase the works of your little artist by dipping alphabet-shaped cookie cutters into paint. Press onto paper; border with fingerpaint smudges around paper's edge.

PARTY

Assemble iron-on fabric letters onto a double-matted strip for an interesting textured title. Adhere sticker strips (Mrs. Grossman's) to background in natural colors.

LEGOS

Nothing makes a statement like the real thing; here thin lego pieces are mounted into letter shapes. Slice paper strips for border; mount around background edge with self-adhesive foam spacers.

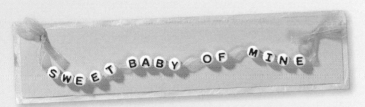

SWEET BABY OF MINE

String a title of alphabet letter beads (The Beadery) on a sheer ribbon (Offray) for a delicate and easy title. Tie into bow at both ends. Mount on mulberry matted background.

Naming the Rabbits

EMBELLISH STENCILED LETTERS

Susan's layered and embellished title lends rustic charm to farm photos. Double mat photo in upper right corner; tear bottom of second mat and adorn with raffia bow. Mat photo to the left; mount eyelets (Impress Rubber Stamps). Tie raffia through eyelets; "hang" on page with small silver brad (Creative Impressions). Mount torn colored paper strip at bottom of page. Cut title letters from stencil (EK Success). Punch small circles with hole punch; add to letters. Intertwine raffia with title letters; mount with self-adhesive foam spacers. Print title and journaling on vellum. Cut to size; layer title strip on chalked bunny die cut. Mount journal block on solid paper with small silver brads. Adhere bunny sticker (Mrs. Grossman's).

Susan Kresge, Temple Terrace, Florida

While we were visiting Grandma's Hug-N-Farm Ryan and Cory spent most of the time petting the rabbits. They loved to catch them and sit and hold them. By the time we left Ryan had all of the little rabbits named. Brownie, Softy and Speedy were a few of the names.

Naming the RABBITS

I Love My Daddy's Shirt

DRESS UP A TITLE

Most of Polly's inspiration comes from everyday life with her daughter, joyfully captured here. Mat patterned paper (Keeping Memories Alive); layer over solid background paper. Cut rectangles; mount down right side of page. Mat photos. Print journaling; cut to size and detail edges with pen. Freehand-write part of title; use template (EK Success) for other portion. Add pen and chalk details to title block; mat on torn paper. Tie jute to buttons; mount small heart button (Hillcreek Designs) on title block. Dangle black buttons with jute from punched holes on text block. Secure buttons to page with self-adhesive foam spacers.

Polly McMillan, Bullhead City, Arizona

Six Ways to Use a Stencil

A stencil creates smooth, evenly spaced letters. It's up to you and your creativity how to decorate them!

Holle Wiktorek, Clarksville, Tennessee

SPRING

Trace and cut out letters from cardstock, outlining edges with blue marker. Embellish using template (C-Thru Ruler) randomly with 3-D stickers (EK Success) and mount on cardstock.

GIFT

Trace and cut out letters from cardstock. Stamp each letter (C-Thru Ruler); color in stamped area with markers. Embellish with handmade "for you" tag.

WEEDING THE GARDEN

Trace and cut out letters using template (C-Thru Ruler), then chalk. Add pen details to letters. Mount on cardstock, print words; draw weeds and chalk to complete.

PARTY

Using a stamp sponge (Tsukineko), pounce ink through stencil (C-Thru Ruler), concentrating on outside edges so they appear darker than the center section. Add pen details and mount on patterned paper then mount again on cardstock.

SNOW

Using chalk, brush through template (C-Thru Ruler), aiming strokes in one direction. Embellish with chalked snowflake punches (Paper Adventures) and double mount on cardstock.

USA

Mount three layers of torn coordinating paper onto cardstock. Trace letters through template (C-Thru Ruler) and cut out. Mount on cardstock.

Down by the Seashore
CUT TITLE LETTERS FROM LARGE STICKER

A large, horizontal sticker was creatively cut and layered into title letters for Lisa's page. Adhere sticker (Sandylion) to white cardstock strip; use Deja Views Spunky lettering template (C-Thru Ruler) for letters. Turn template over and trace letters backward on back of cardstock strip; cut out letters, paper tearing their tops. Cut title letters again from blue paper; layer and mount torn letter over blue letter. Mount small title letters on paper rectangles; detail with black pen. Tear white paper strips; mount. Adhere horizontal sticker onto blue cardstock strip; mount over white torn paper strip. Double mat photos. Mat journaling; adhere sticker letters (MAMBI) on journaling block. Make grid of string and brads (Making Memories) to link everything together.

Lisa Dixon, East Brunswick, New Jersey

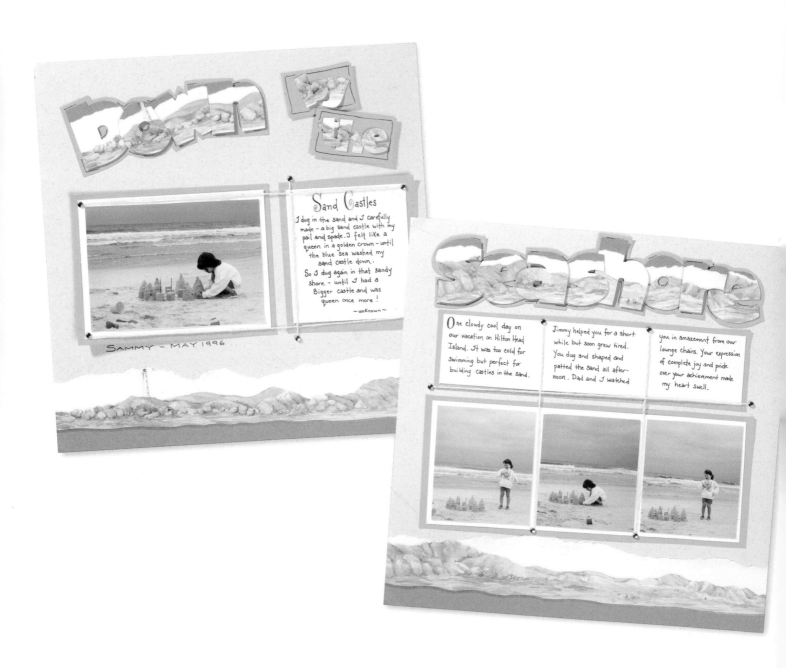

Heartbreaker

ADHERE A STICKER TITLE

Serafina captures the essence of her daughter's spirit with a one-word title. Layer solid-colored rectangle over patterned background paper (Scrap in a Snap). Adhere sticker letter title (Stickopotamus). Print journaling on vellum; adhere to page and embellish with pink ribbon (Stampin' Up!). Mat photos on opposite page on solid paper; mount over torn paper strip. Add heart buttons (source unknown) and ribbon embellishments.

Serafina Andolina,
Schenectady, New York

Summer Blocks

PUNCH SQUARES FOR TITLE LETTERS

Reeca's monochromatic color scheme gives warmth to an enlarged photo of her daughter. Cut one square of four complementary patterned papers (Provo Craft); adhere to page in quadrants. Punch squares in two sizes (Creative Memories) for title letters; layer as shown. Adhere sticker letters (EK Success) to squares. Chalk edges of sun die cut (Pebbles in My Pocket); mount. Print journaling; trim to size and mat. Add chalk details to highlight text and edges of text block. Punch small sun (EK Success); mount on small punched and matted square with eyelets (Doodlebug Design).

Reeca Davis Marotz, Idaho Falls, Idaho

Borders

Borders are the upper, lower and vertical edges of a scrapbook page. Decorative borders are design elements that embrace sections of a page, adding a portion of a frame. Borders can be made with creatively placed photos, punched shapes, stickers, color blocking or fibers to add quick and simple zip to any layout.

Happy Holidays
PIECE TOGETHER A PHOTO BORDER

Lisa highlights each child's unique personality on an eye-catching photo border. Double mat large photo on patterned paper (Mercer Motifs). Mount on matted color-blocked background. Adhere title sticker (Mercer Motifs) on patterned paper strip. Print photo captions onto patterned paper; cut to size. Mount on bottom border strip with cropped photos.

Lisa Kaelberer, Chyops, Bountiful, Utah

Beach Babes
SLICE A PHOTO BORDER

Simple slices of green paper accent Tammy's grassy seaside photos. Slice an enlarged photo at random intervals; mount at bottom of page leaving space between each slice to give the illusion of a panoramic photo. Mat photo; mount on speckled background paper (Bazzill). Slice thin, curved strips of green paper to resemble blades of grass; mount on page as shown. Print title and poem on vellum; add starfish nailhead (Jest Charming) and decorative shaker box (EK Success).

Tammy Gauck, Jenison, Michigan

When in Drought
PIECE TOGETHER A PHOTO BORDER

Torrey's photo border gives the illusion of a single panoramic photo, but is in fact the same photo duplicated and "spliced" together. Print title on solid-colored paper, tear into strips and layer on page. Single, double and triple mat photos. Hang sunflower charms (Charming Pages) from handmade wire (Artistic Wire) swirls. Print journaling on vellum; trim to size and run through Xyron machine before adhering over photo. Stamp sunflower (PSX) and silhouette shape; mount on title strip using foam spacers for added dimension.

Torrey Miller, Westminster, Colorado

Megan

PUNCH A GEOMETRIC BORDER

Angie assembled this portrait page of her daughter in less than 15 minutes
with the help of geometric-shaped punches. Mat photo; cut photo corners
with decorative scissors (Provo Craft). Punch eight "v" shapes with chevron
punch (Family Treasures) from coordinating patterned papers (Paper
Adventures) for each border. Mount on page as shown. Punch squares for
center of borders and title letters. Adhere sticker letters (Paper Adventures)
for title.

Angie Villandre, Westfield, Indiana

Daddy and Jarod

PUNCH A DELICATE BORDER DESIGN

A punched border from patterned paper gives a lacy look to Tracie's page. Double mat photo on patterned paper (Scrap Ease); mount on background paper. Slice border strips from patterned papers; trim one strip with decorative scissors. Use border punch (Emagination Crafts) on other paper strip. Steps for creating a neat continuous border are shown below. Layer both strips on left side of page as shown. Print title onto vellum (Paper Adventures). Paper tear to size and mount. Punch heart (Punch Bunch); tie fiber (source unknown) into bow and mount on heart.

Tracie Zody, Richmond, Virginia

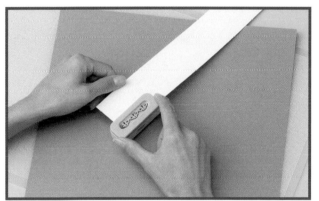

1 Punch the first design on edge of paper.

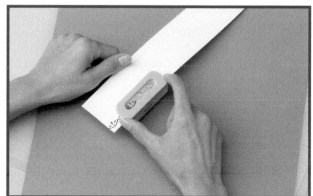

2 To create continuous borders, align edge of punch so patterns overlap. The end of your first punch pattern should overlap with the beginning of your second.

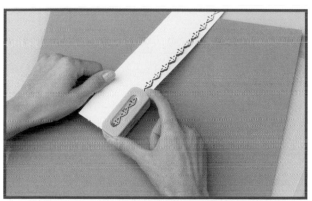

3 Continue punching down the edge of paper until the border is complete.

Among the Giants
ADD DIMENSION TO A STICKER BORDER

Large tree stickers are layered with foam spacers to add dimension to Kelly's paper-torn border. Paper tear monochromatic strips; layer and attach with eyelets. Adhere tree stickers (Provo Craft) to ivory cardstock; silhouette-cut around image. Layer on paper-torn border with self-adhesive foam spacers. String hemp cord through eyelets; secure at back of page. Double mat photos with solid and patterned (Scrap Ease) papers; mount. Adhere sticker letters (Debbie Mumm, Creative Imaginations).

Kelly Angard, Highlands Ranch, Colorado

Quick Tip: Instead of spending a ton of money on new lettering stickers, improvise with your leftovers: With a little creative rearranging, a backward "3" becomes an "E," an upside down "7" becomes an "L," and a trimmed "O" becomes a "C." Bonus: You might even stumble upon a new font!

Shades of Fall
CRAFT A DIMENSIONAL STICKER BORDER

Trudy's rustic, dimensional border is topped with colorful leaf stickers that look authentically real. Layer solid papers for background. Tear paper strips for borders at top and bottom of page; mount strips of twine (Earth Goods) on top. Cut 1½" and 2" squares; crumple paper and wrap with twine before matting. Adhere leaf stickers (Creative Imaginations); mount squares over border strips. Print title and journaling; cut to size and mat. Complete page by matting photos and adding small leaf stickers to journaling block.

Trudy Sigurdson, Victoria, BC, Canada

Sticker Borders

Add oomph to borders with artistic, versatile and easy-to-apply stickers. Layer, cut, scene build and much more!

Trudy Sigurdson, Victoria, BC, Canada

SEASHELL

Build a dimensional sticker border with a strip of seashell stickers (Provo Craft) cut into squares and reassembled. Mount on double-matted border strip with self-adhesive foam spacers.

BUTTERFLIES

Colorful butterflies look as if they're about to take flight because of a clever dimensional layering technique. Mount butterfly stickers (Colorbök) on border strip. Punch square shape into butterfly. Mat square on solid-colored paper; mount over punched area with self-adhesive foam spacers.

FLOWERS

Tulip bulbs burst into full bloom from layered torn paper strips. Gently slice leaves from stems on flower stickers (Provo Craft); dust sticky side with powder to remove tackiness; set aside. Adhere flowers to torn paper strip. Mount with self-adhesive foam spacers. Add another torn paper strip across the bottom using self-adhesive foam spacers.

DAISY

Delicate daisy stickers (Frances Meyer) are mounted on double-matted rectangles and tied with sheer ribbon bows to matting. Use this easy idea with a variety of stickers and fibers to match the theme of your page.

SNOWFLAKES

Sheer vellum snowflake stickers dusted with powder (Autumn Leaves) keep their translucent beauty while mounted on blue-and-white fiber strands (On The Surface) with self-adhesive foam spacers.

CHRISTMAS LIGHTS

Add a string of snow-covered Christmas lights to a holiday border with sheer sticker bulbs dusted with powder (Provo Craft) and mounted with self-adhesive foam spacers. Slice wavy border from white cardstock; decorate with shaved ice (Magic Scraps) to give a sparkly, snowy effect.

The Great Toilet Paper Caper

ZIG ZAG A SOFT FIBER BORDER

Andrea captured the chaos of a toddler's curious mind with a comical title and dimensional border. For left page, vertically tear solid green paper; mount white brads (Hyglo/American Pin) 1½" apart on each side. Adhere torn paper over patterned paper (Colors by Design) with self-adhesive foam spacers. Zig zag chenille fiber (Lion Brand Yarn), securing under brads. Mat photo on large rectangle, leaving room for title block. Print title in various fonts and colors. Cut to size and block together. For right page, tear patterned paper and mount as a border. Mount photos. Print journaling; cut to size and mat, tearing bottom.

Andrea Hautala, Olympia, Washington

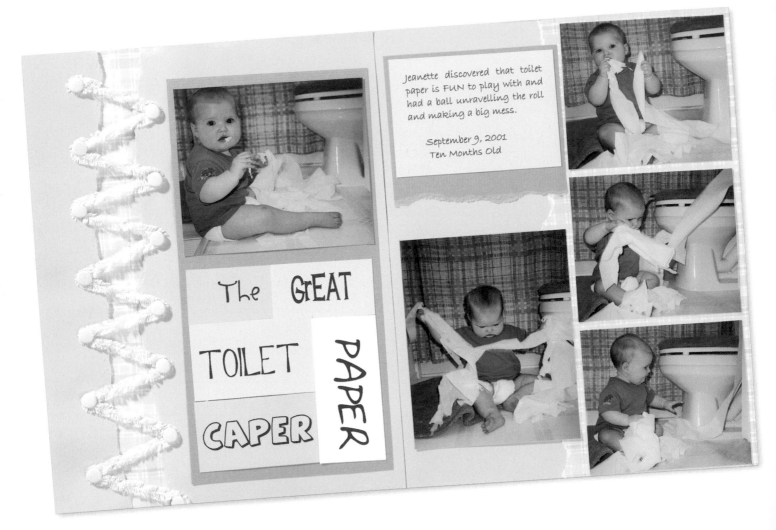

> **Quick Tip:** Avoid repeating the same old words over and over and over and over again. Pick up a thesaurus (or use one available on your computer) to track down fresh words that convey similar meanings. Your journaling will become vibrantly more interesting.

Forever

WRAP A SOFT FIBER BORDER

Holly wanted to make sure attention wasn't detracted from a treasured photo, so she opted for a simple layout with short, concise journaling. Mat photo on solid paper; mount on speckled background paper. Print title and journaling on white paper; cut to size. Color title letters with colored pencils. Mat on solid paper torn at the top before mounting on page. Create a soft border by wrapping chenille strands (Lion Brand Yarn) around the bottom of the page. Make your fiber border more stable by following the steps illustrated below. Tie into a bow to secure.

Holly Van Dyne, Mansfield, Ohio
Photos, Keepsake Photography, Mansfield, Ohio

1 Cut approximately ⅛" notch where you want your fibers to start.

2 On back side, thread fibers through the notch and attach with an adhesive or double-sided tape.

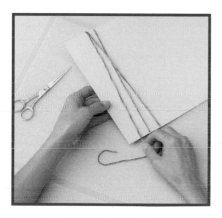

3 Continue notching edges as you wind fiber around to create border. Attach at end or tie into a bow.

Yoda

LINE UP A COLOR-BLOCKED BORDER

Tara features her cat's unique personality with a journaling block full of precious pet nicknames. Create a quick and easy border of monochromatic colors by cutting 1 x 4" rectangles; mount down left side of page. Mat photos; mount on page. Print journaling; cut to size. Mat die-cut letters (Ellison/Provo Craft); silhouette cut.

Tara Gangi, Hewitt, New Jersey

Giraffe

ASSEMBLE A COLOR-BLOCKED BORDER

Oksanna assembled a visually interesting color-blocked border from a variety of solid and patterned papers. Cut rectangles in various lengths and widths; layer at top of patterned background paper (Karen Foster Design). Cut title letters from two templates (EZ2Cut, C-Thru Ruler); mount over color-blocked border. Double and triple mat photos; detail with hand-drawn design around second mat of one photo. Stamp ethnic designs (All Night Media); cut to size and double mat. Tie fiber (Adornaments by EK Success) at center of stamped design and mount. Adhere corrugated die-cut giraffe (DMD).

Oksanna Pope, Los Gatos, California

My Special Balloon

COLOR BLOCK A GEOMETRIC BORDER

Trudy assembled a monochromatic geometric border to offset soft floral details. Print title and journaling onto white paper; mat and mount on matted background paper. Mount enlarged photo. See the steps below to make this striking border. Before adhering daisy stickers (Paper House Productions) with self-adhesive foam spacers, lightly dust back of sticker with small brush dipped in baby powder to prevent sticker from adhering to page.

Trudy Sigurdson, Victoria, BC, Canada

1 Cut or punch:
3 white squares 1¼ x 1¼"
3 light purple squares 1½ x 1½"
4 light purple rectangles 2¾ x ½"
6 medium purple rectangles
½ x 2⅛"
6 dark purple rectangles ½ x ⅛"

2 Assemble rectangles and squares along vertical border as shown. Adhere.

3 Adhere sunflower stickers to center of each square with self-adhesive foam spacers.

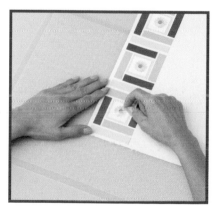

Mats

Matting, the act of attaching a piece of paper to the back of a photo before mounting the shot, helps a picture visually jump off a page. It separates the photo from other page elements by providing an island or frame for the shot. Mats can be simplistic or highly adorned with ribbons, fabric, torn paper and three-dimensional embellishments.

McCoy, Megan and Hannah

FRAME A PHOTO WITH A VELLUM OVERLAY

Katie focuses on a favorite photo by creating a vellum overlay "window" to achieve a frosted-looking frame. Mat photo on solid paper; add curves using a decorative ruler as a guide. Cut vellum "window" with a craft knife. Print title and text; trim to size and cut vellum "windows." Punch shapes (EK Success) from vellum and solid papers. Hang shapes from title block and across bottom of page with embroidery floss (Designs for the Needle).

Katie Swanson, South Milwaukee, Wisconsin

Jetty Park

I love...
the sounds
of the beach.
The seagulls,
the waves,
the children
laughing.
I love...
walking slowly
through the
water and
picking up
tiny seashells.
I love...
making
sandcastles
with dripping,
wet sand.

I have been going to
Jetty Park with my
family since I was a
very young girl. It
was nice to be able
to visit with my family.
The wild cats are
still there eating fish
and there are always
ships going in and
out of the canal.
Sometimes we are
able to watch rockets
at Cape Canaveral.

Jetty Park

STACK PHOTOS ON MATTING

Antuanette's paper-torn matting provides the perfect look for a trio of seaside photos. Mat three photos on one large piece of solid-colored paper; tear one side of matting. Double mat photo for left page; tear one side of first mat. Mount satin ribbon (Offray) horizontally at top and bottom of pages. Print title letters; silhouette-cut with craft knife. Layer over vellum strip before mounting. Print journaling onto vellum; cut to size. Layer vellum over small paper strips to highlight words in text block. Adhere sea-related stickers (Debbie Mumm).

Antuanette Wheeler, Center Hill, Florida

Chris

TEAR A COLOR-BLOCKED PHOTO MAT

Jodi combines paper tearing and color blocking to make a colorful photo mat for her page. Tear varying-length paper strips in two colors; layer at bottom of page over matted, patterned background paper (Scrapbook Wizard). Mount Sizzix die-cut letters and stars (Ellison/ Provo Craft) to paper strip and background paper; detail letters and stars with black pen. Tie buttons with pearlized thread (DMC); mount on stars. Mat photos together. Follow the steps below to create the colorful blocked mat. Tear paper square for journaling block; write with black pen.

Jodi Amidei, Memory Makers

Photos, Diane Amidei, Erie, Colorado

1 Tear various rectangle shapes in three different colors of cardstock.

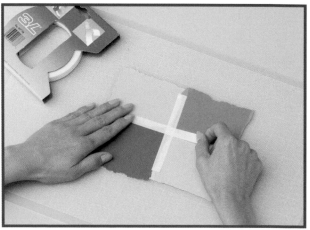

2 Adhere all four pieces together on backside with photo tape.

Zest

COLOR BLOCK A FUNKY FRAME

Kelli's funky, color-blocked photo frame seems to jump off the page thanks to its wavy design and dimensional mounting. Use wavy cutting system (Creative Memories) to cut strips of monochromatic paper; mount together using double-sided tape. Trim frame edges and cut window with craft knife. Mount over photo with self-adhesive foam spacers. Freehand-draw and cut title letters; mat and silhouette cut. Mount with self-adhesive foam spacers. Print journaling; cut to size and mount.

Kelli Noto, Centennial, Colorado

Name

ADD INTEREST TO PHOTO MATS

Oksanna's adorned photo mats add visual interest to a simple, elegant layout. Print journaling on patterned (EK Success) and solid papers. Layer patterned paper (EK Success) over solid paper for background. Triple mat photo on upper page slightly askew; add freehand design on third matting with black pen. Double mat photo on right page; stamp dragonfly (All Night Media) on two edges of second matting. Add details with gold dimensional paint (Duncan). Adhere title letter stickers (C-Thru Ruler).

Oksanna Pope, Los Gatos, California

Best Friends

EMBELLISH PHOTO MATS

Trudy's triple-matted photo is highlighted with metal title letters and simple embellishments. Layer subtle patterned paper (Karen Foster Design) over solid paper. Print journaling on solid paper. Paper tear wide strips; embellish with eyelets (Eyelet Factory) and buttons (Making Memories) before mounting on background. Triple-mat photo; tear sides of second mat and add embellishments as shown. Attach metal title letters (Making Memories) with eyelets to second mat.

Trudy Sigurdson, Victoria, BC, Canada

Six Ways to Adorn Your Mat

Make your mat matter with torn paper, ribbons, eyelets and other supplies that turn a plain mat into a work of art.

Valerie Barton, Flowood, Mississippi

BLUE

Torn paper strips layered horizontally and vertically over a matted photo provide a creative way to cover the date stamp on a photo.

ORANGE

Nestle a photo under an embellished fold-over mat. Cut second mat 1 to 2" larger than first. Score paper with bone folder; tear edge of matting before folding over photo. Mount die-cut leaves (Dayco); embellish with chalk (Craf-T).

GREEN WITH YELLOW RIBBON

String ribbon through eyelets for a charming way to frame a photo. Attach eyelets (Doodlebug Design) on mat as shown; weave ribbon through eyelets, securing at back of matting.

PURPLE

Weave thin paper strips at corners for an interesting and dimensional photo frame. Slice 12¼" paper strips. Mount strips to matting around photo; weave with under/over technique at corners.

TURQUOISE/ORANGE

Embellish paper-torn matting with a string of colored buttons. Mat photo; tear horizontally at bottom and mat again. String buttons (Making Memories) on fiber (On The Surface). Mount diagonally at upper left corner; secure at back of matting.

OLIVE GREEN

Lace a fold-over mat with hemp cord to add a rustic feel to photo mats. Punch small shape through fold-over matting; lace hemp cord (Westrim Crafts) through holes and secure on back of matting.

· A Mothers pride ·

Alex, you bring more joy to my life than you will ever know. You are a sweet, loving & sensitive child & I hope you never loose those wonderful qualities

My heart is filled with such love when you tell me that I am prettier than a sunset and more cuddly than your teddy bear. I will love you forever.

I love it when you want to sit close to me and cuddle, and it really touches my heart when you come up to me wanting to give me hugs and kisses just because.

When you were born & I found out I had a son, I didn't know what I was going to do with a boy. But now I know that all I need to do is to love you.

· a l e x ·   · july first ·

· two thousand one ·

Chapter 4
Embellishments

Whether your favorite outfit is a gorgeous red gown, a simple black dress or a knockout silk suit, it's not complete without accessories. It doesn't take much dressing up to turn stunning into spectacular, just a pair of diamond earrings or a slender gold necklace! And, just as accessories make an outfit, embellishments add that extra *je ne sais quoi* to your scrapbook page.

Scrapbook embellishments range from very simple pre-made to extremely extravagant handmade. The type and portion of embellishments you add to your pages speaks worlds about your personal flair. From photo tags, stamped borders, beaded titles and vellum matting, to ribbon edgings and paper-pieced hearts and flowers, you'll find a showcase of ideas within this chapter to help you dress up your scrapbook spreads.

Pre-Made Embellishments

Stop by your local craft or scrapbook store and you'll find racks of pre-made embellishments. They are created to move straight out of the package and onto your scrapbook page. Pre-made embellishments come in thousands of theme and color schemes. Just place and admire.

I Can Tie My Shoes!

ACCENT DIE CUTS WITH REALISTIC DETAILS

Melissa illustrates her daughter's new achievement with realistic-looking laser die cuts. Mat photos on a 4" wide strip of white paper, leaving room in the middle for journaling. Cut journaling block; mount with eyelets (Impress Rubber Stamps) and tie with string. Mount on left side of page over patterned background paper (Making Memories). Double mat large photo. Assemble tennis shoe die cuts (Deluxe Cuts); detail with chalk (Craf-T), eyelets and string. Adhere title sticker letters (Provo Craft) and matted paper rectangle.

Melissa Ackerman, Princeton, New Jersey

Just Fishing

ASSEMBLE A COLLECTION OF PRE-MADE ACCESSORIES

Jill accents heritage photos with a charming collection of fishing accessories. Double mat speckled background paper. Cut wavy background from patterned paper (source unknown); mount along bottom of page. Punch green plants (Family Treasures); layer on page. Adhere pre-made fishing accessories (EK Success). Mat photos; mount on page. Cut title letters from template (EK Success). Print journaling; cut to size, mat and mount.

Jill Cornelius, Allen, Texas

Mom & I

COLLAGE PRE-MADE EMBELLISHMENTS

Torrey gives pre printed embellishments a new look by creating a collage of dimensional images. Paper tear strips of solid-colored paper; mount diagonally on opposite corners. Cut large square of red paper with decorative scissors; mount at center of background paper, slightly askew. Mat and layer photos. Cut apart pre printed embellishments (EK Success) with regular and decorative scissors. Casually arrange on page, mounting some with self-adhesive foam spacers. Print journaling; cut to size and mount.

Torrey Miller, Westminster, Colorado

Paper-Torn Embellishing

Tear paper into strips or shapes and reassemble to create pictures or patterns. Paper tearing can be applied to paper of all textures and colors. Use a pattern, or freehand tear and apply the pieces in mosaic or collage patterns. The choice is yours.

This was the first year that Robby carved his own pumpkin. Oliver was so proud of his big brother so he wanted to take his picture with it.

First Carving

CRAFT A PAPER-TORN PUMPKIN

Shannon crafted her own seasonal masterpiece out of small pieces of torn paper. This easy technique is achieved by tearing small pieces of complementary-colored paper and then layering them into a desired shape. It may be helpful to first sketch the shape onto background paper to serve as a guide. Add chalk and pen lines for depth and definition once placement is complete. Double mat photos; layer over torn paper strip. Cut title letters using template (EK Success). Journal on torn paper strip.

Shannon Taylor, Bristol, Tennessee

By the Sea

PAPER-TEAR A SEASIDE SCENE

Beverly's use of color and texture sets the tone for a peaceful seaside scene. Mat photos on solid paper torn on two sides and chalk around all edges. Add eyelets (Club Scrap) at corners and layer over torn mulberry paper before mounting on patterned background paper (Club Scrap). Cut palm tree and sun from templates (C-Thru Ruler). Paper tear shapes and run through crimper (Fiskars) for texture. Chalk around edges for added depth; layer sun over torn mulberry. Handcraft tags; add eyelets and mulberry strips before layering. Print text. Cut title and text blocks; chalk around edges before layering on tags.

Beverly Sizemore, Sulligent, Alabama

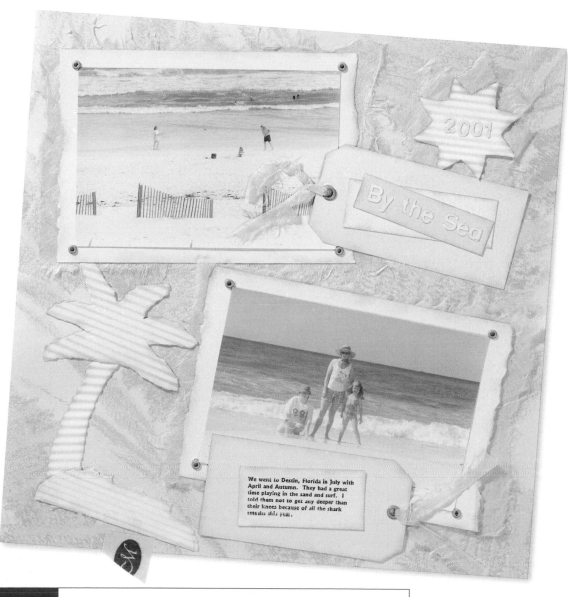

Quick Tip: For smoother results, use a paintbrush dipped lightly in water to outline paper shapes before tearing them.

Sticker Embellishing

It's easy as pie to add a splash of color, whimsy or grace to a page using stickers. Available in a rainbow of colors and an endless variety of themes, stickers are a speedy antidote for any humdrum page.

God Bless America

SHOW SPIRIT WITH PATRIOTIC STICKERS

Jennifer adorns her patriotic page with seasonal stickers that show her true Fourth of July spirit. Double mat red paper for background. Double mat photo. Print journaling; mat and adhere sticker kids (EK Success). Cut title block to size and mat; adhere "America" sticker (EK Success) and small black sticker letters (Provo Craft). Adhere firecracker and star stickers (EK Success).

Jennifer Blackham, West Jordan, Utah

All Grown Up

ADD CHARM WITH SILHOUETTE STICKERS

Lori's monochromatic heritage layout is elegantly highlighted with a simple silhouette sticker border. Slice solid paper strip; mount over patterned paper (EK Success) at right. Cut rectangles from solid paper; adhere silhouette stickers (Okie-Dokie Press) before mounting on paper strip. Mat large photo; mount on page. Print title onto vellum; cut to size and double mat. Adhere flower sticker (Okie-Dokie Press).

Lori Streich, Sioux Falls, South Dakota

Hit the Trail
ADHERE A STICKER TITLE

Jennifer chooses to anchor sticker accents to paper strips so they aren't floating on her page. Slice large photo at random intervals; mount on cardstock, leaving space between each slice. Print journaling on solid-colored paper; mat and mount on matted patterned background paper (Rocky Mountain Scrapbook Co.). Mat photos; mount. Slice two strips of colored cardstock; adhere stickers (Karen Foster Design) and attach small brad (Impress Rubber Stamps). Adhere sticker title (Karen Foster Design) and hiking boots on journaling block to solidify theme.

Jennifer Blackham, West Jordan, Utah

Quick Tip: Once a month, get your friends together for a scrapbook supply swap. Invite your guests to bring along their leftover stickers, paper scraps, stamps, (that adorable firefighter paper doll you bought three years ago but haven't yet used)—and trade with each other. Remember, one person's junk is another scrapbooker's treasure!

Chalk Embellishing

Chalk, that schoolyard staple, has made its way to scrapbooking. Use it to colorize torn-paper edges, die cuts, journaling blocks and other elements, adding highlights and dimension.

You Color My World

CHALK A RAINBOW BORDER

Christina couldn't resist using bright ponytail bands as a perfect page embellishment. Tear edges of patterned paper (Mustard Moon), chalking around them in various colors to give a rainbow effect. Mount on patterned paper (Mustard Moon). Print part of title and journaling on vellum and patterned papers. Cut title block to size and mat on patterned paper. Cut large title letters from template (Scrap Pagerz) and a variety of patterned papers. Add eyelets (Doodlebug Design) to letters before mounting on title block with self-adhesive foam spacers. Tear edges of journal block and chalk (Craf-T). Layer over patterned paper strips. Mount looped ponytail bands to page.

Christina Gibson, Jonesboro, Arkansas

Summer

DRESS UP TEMPLATE LETTERS

Victoria illustrates the sandy shades of summer with heavily chalked torn paper and title letters. Mat photos before layering on page. Tear speckled paper; chalk heavily, as shown in illustrations below, with various shades of brown to resemble sand colors in photos. Layer at bottom of page. Cut title letters from template (Provo Craft); outline with black pen and shade with chalk before matting on black paper. Silhouette-cut letters before mounting on page. Paper tear sun; journal with black pen.

Victoria Jiminez, Harrah, Oklahoma

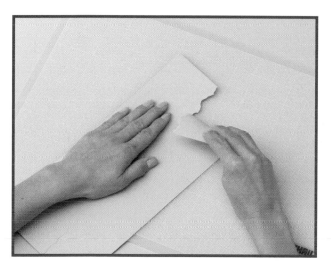

1 Tear border from a sheet of sand-colored paper. Steady the sheet with one hand while using the other to carefully rip the page from top to bottom.

2 Using chalk and a cotton swab, gently rub chalk on torn edge to add dimension, texture and color.

Quick Tip: To save money, substitute any non-oily, powder-based makeup like eye shadow or blush for chalk on your pages.

Punch and Die-Cut Embellishing

Punches, those individual paper cutting tools that create perfect decorative shapes, are just right for dressing up borders, corners, titles and much more. Layer them or use them alone for "wow" effects.

Pumpkins

PUNCH A PLAYFUL BORDER

Jenna knows that scrapbooking inspiration can be found anywhere—even bathroom floors! The variety of punched circles shown here are the product of Jenna's never-ending search for great ideas. Mat photos on solid-colored paper. Punch a variety of circle sizes (½", ¾", Marvy; 1", Family Treasures) out of complementary-colored papers. Cut title letters using template (Scrap Pagerz). Cut larger circles with circle cutter.

Jenna Beegle, Woodstock, Georgia

Big Adventure

DANGLE A TAG IN YOUR TITLE

Janice's choice of warm, patterned papers provides an understated background for black-and-white photos. Cut green paper (EK Success) in half; mount over yellow paper (EK Success). Slice paper strip; mount at top left of page. Cut circle from patterned paper (Avery); adhere sticker letters (Provo Craft). Dangle tag from loop tied in embroidery floss (DMC); mount horizontally, securing to page back. Print partial title and journaling on vellum. Cut balance of title. Cut suns using templates (EK Success); mount on matted squares of patterned paper.

Janice Carson, Hamilton, ON, Canada

Dress Up Punches

Punched shapes are great embellishments in and of themselves, but dress them up and they go from simple to sensational.

Holle Wiktorek, Fayetteville, North Carolina

Nestle a punched star (Marvy) amongst tinseled strands (Magic Scraps) for a glittery effect.

Add eyelets to a paper-torn sunflower's center; surround with punched petals (EK Success).

Punch a heart silhouette (EK Success) from aluminum to frame a small photo. Embellish with twisted wire (Artistic Wire) at top of tag.

Add pen detail to a simple punched starburst (EK Success) before mounting on torn paper strip.

A small button (Making Memories) adorns a bright punched sun (Marvy). Mount eyelet (Making Memories) on tag and tie with hemp cord.

Wrap a punched maple leaf (Marvy) with thin wire (Artistic Wire) before mounting with self-adhesive foam spacers.

Give texture and visual interest to punches with mesh (Avant Card). Adhere mesh to cardstock before punching tree (EK Success). Layer shape over paper-torn scrap. If using thicker mesh, simply punch shape from cardstock first, then adhere mesh under shape.

Pen and chalk details give dimension to a punched birch leaf (Marvy). Mount on printed vellum (EK Success); tear edges before mounting on handmade tag. Attach star eyelet (Stamp Doctor) and raffia.

Adorn a heart-shaped punch (Marvy) with a plastic safety pin and pen detail to enhance baby-themed artwork.

Punch a window into a tag, small envelope or a border strip for a charming view. Add clear jewels (Westrim) to punched snowflakes (Crafts, Etc.); mount under punched window.

Stamp Embellishing

Rubber stamps are versatile tools for adding spark to scrapbook pages. With thousands of patterns and inks in a rainbow of colors, you can create delicate borders, lacy corners, dressed-up die cuts and jazzy page accents.

Together

ADD SHINE WITH METAL WORD EYELETS

Lisa's simple border incorporates a stamped design with metal word eyelets. Print title and journaling. Mount photo on journaling block and mat. Cut title to size; mat and mount with self-adhesive foam spacers. Stamp sun designs (DeNami Design) on background paper. Mount word eyelets (Making Memories) over stamped design.

Lisa Simon, Roanoke, Virginia

Pure Wonder

STAMP A SIMPLE DESIGN

Anne's goal of creating a simple, clean page was met by using a variety of embellishments. Single and double mat photos. Attach eyelets (Stamp Doctor) to bottom of matting; thread fiber (Rubba Dub Dub) through eyelets. Layer over patterned paper (Paper Loft) and mat. Print title and journaling; cut to size and mount. Hand cut large word for title. Attach eyelets at top and bottom of opposite page, threading fiber through. Cut rectangles from solid paper; mat with dark paper. Stamp leaf (Stampin' Up!) and shadow square (Hero Arts). Attach eyelets and fibers.

Anne Heyen, New Fairfield, Connecticut

Kindness

LACE A STAMPED BORDER

Oksanna cut out stamped images of peaches and laced them together with ribbon for a simple, fanciful border that complements her page's theme. Print journaling onto vellum (DMD); mount vellum rectangles over patterned paper (Carolee's Creations). Mat two photos. Stamp peaches (All Night Media) on solid paper; cut to size with decorative scissors. Punch (Fiskars) small holes in stamped images; lace ribbon (Offray) through and arrange as shown. Cut title from template (EZ2Cut) in two colors; layer on page to create shadow effect. Complete title with black pen.

Oksanna Pope, Los Gatos, California

Autumn Days

DANGLE EMBOSSED STAMPED IMAGES

Falling leaves drift peacefully along Heidi's color-blocked border. Punch small squares (Family Treasures) and leaves (EK Success) from complementary solid-colored papers. Slice corrugated paper strip; mount. Cut title letters from template (Frances Meyer); overlap and mount. Follow the instructions below to emboss the large leaf accents and add buttons; mount on title strip. Mount cropped photos. Hand write balance of title on paper strip; punch small hole and tie hemp cord (Darice). Mount with self-adhesive foam spacers.

Heidi Schueller, Waukesha, Wisconsin

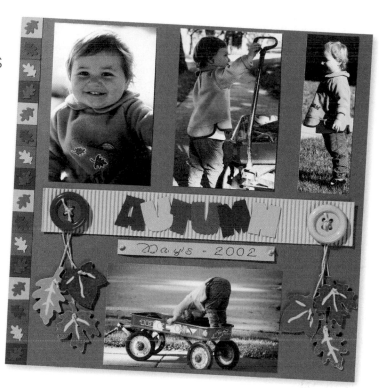

1 Stamp image on cardstock, being careful to press the stamp firmly and evenly on the paper. Do not rock.

2 Lightly sprinkle clear embossing powder over stamped image. Take care to cover all of the image evenly.

3 Use heat gun to melt powder.

4 Cut out embossed images. Punch small holes and attach hemp, knotting at front of leaves. Tie cords together; attach to buttons.

Tag Embellishing

Tags are available in many sizes, colors and shapes. Use them as embellishments in your page design or as platforms for titles and journaling. Spruce them up or dress them down as you desire.

Sam's Fishing Hat

ADD SIMPLE EMBELLISHMENTS TO TAGS

Kathy's clean lines and simple tag embellishments keep the focus of her page on the color-tinted black-and white photo. Double mat photo; layer on patterned paper (source unknown) embellished with eyelets (Stamp Doctor) and embroidery thread (On The Surface). Print journaling; trim to size and mat. Slice paper strip for title; adhere sticker letters (Making Memories) and mat. Embellish tags (Avery) with patterned paper, punched shapes (McGill) and embroidery thread.

Kathy Olson, Madison, Wisconsin

Our Daughters

ADORN TAGS WITH PAPER SCRAPS

Embellished tags tied with ribbon and adorned with jewels add charm to Kelly's page. Divide page into four sections; cut solid and patterned (Treehouse Designs) paper to fit sections. Mount on solid-colored paper, leaving space between each section. Color block mat for top photo; tie ribbon around matted photo. Double and quadruple mat bottom photos on solid and patterned papers. Cut photo corners with decorative scissors; mount. Wrap fibers (Making Memories) on opposite corners. Embellish tags with paper scraps; adhere title sticker letters (MAMBI). Mount flat-backed jewels (Magic Scraps) and chalk around edges. Tie ribbon and fibers on tags.

Kelly Angard, Highlands Ranch, Colorado
Photos, Stacey Heckert, Highlands Ranch, Colorado

Fiber Embellishing

Fiber, ribbon, string, thread, yarn, floss, jute and other textiles are increasingly popular with scrapbookers. Use them to suspend titles, wind around borders or decorate other page elements such as tags and frames.

Today You Are You

FRAME A PHOTO WITH RIBBON

Jane captures the sweet essence of her daughter with a photo delicately framed with sheer ribbon and flower nailheads. Tear patterned and embossed vellum (K & Company); mount at lower left-hand corner of page. Mount photos on page. Frame one photo by attaching sheer ribbon (Stampin' Up!) with flower nailheads (Jest Charming) at corners. Print text onto vellum; tear edges and mount on page. Affix nailheads to complete page.

Jane Rife, Hendersonville, Tennessee

Lauren

ADD A FEMININE BORDER

Valerie surrounds a sweet photo of her daughter with strips of delicate satin and sheer ribbon. Double mat photo. Cut title from computer-printed font with craft knife. Mount ribbon (Offray) to page as shown, wrapping ends around the back of the page. Hand cut tag; punch hole and embellish with pressed flowers and ribbon.

Valerie Simon, Carmel, Indiana

Cunningham Falls State Park
SECURE EMBELLISHMENTS WITH FIBERS

Tina's first experience with the sights and sounds of fall is elegantly displayed with realistic embellishments. Mat photos on solid-colored paper; tear two edges. Mat largest photo; attach eyelets (Making Memories) and string fiber (On The Surface) vertically on matting. Cut rectangles to mat skeleton leaves (Graphic Products Corp.) upon; attach eyelets and crisscross fibers over leaf. Print journaling, leaving room for highlighted sticker words. Adhere sticker letters (Creative Memories); cut to size and tear. Paper tear title strip; adhere sticker letters (Colorbök).

Tina Kistinger, Pasadena, California

Fiber Embellishments

Yarn, thread, hemp and other fibers add texture and dimension to tags, titles, borders and other elements.

Kelli Noto, Centennial, Colorado

UNDER THE SEA:

Metallic and cotton fibers frayed at the edges replicate underwater plant life. Punch letters (EK Success); mount on matted background paper. Tear thin cork for bottom of sea. Adhere fish stickers (Stickopotamus). Cut large and small fiber strips (Magic Scraps); fray edges and mount.

CELESTIAL TAG:

A soft combination of fibers (On The Fringe, Magic Scraps) in natural colors adds interest to a distressed tag. Stamp tag with celestial design (Rubber Stamps Of America); ink background and detail edges. Crumple tag and flatten out before tying fibers.

STITCHED FLOWERS:

Add homemade charm to borders with hand-stitched flowers. Lightly pencil flower shape; pierce holes with hole piercer before stitching. Mount button tied with fiber. Double mat designs.

FACES:

Trim fibers into the perfect hairstyle to frame faces of all cultures. Cut or punch ovals and circles for faces. Detail with pen and chalk; mount eyes. Cut fibers (Quilter's Resource Inc., DMC, EK Success) for hair; mount.

CACTUS:

Detail cactus die-cuts with realistic-looking prickles. Punch small holes in die cuts; tie fibers through holes.

STAR:

Decorative rickrack threaded through large eyelets makes for a colorful, eye-catching embellishment. Mount large eyelets (Darice) at points of star. Thread rickrack (Magic Scraps) through eyelets in shape of star.

Wire Embellishing

Solid, stiff and strong, wires can add a masculine feel to your scrapbook pages. When threaded with beads, or strung with ribbons or floral punches, wire can easily drift from rustic to elegant. The beauty of wire is its flexibility.

The Magic of Music City

DANGLE WIRE MUSICAL NOTES

In order to keep her page from looking too formal, Jessica added whimsical wire "jewelry" creatively shaped into musical notes. Double mat photos; mount on page. Print title and journaling onto vellum. Cut to size; mount over solid-colored paper strips. Embellish with wire (Darice) and bead (Halcraft) designs; mount with adhesive, as shown below.

Jessica Mobley, Thompson Station, Tennessee

1 With round-tip pliers, bend wire into desired shape, adding beads as desired.

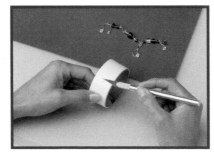

2 Pick up glue dot with the tip of a craft knife.

3 Adhere glue dot to a bead and place the bead on the page. Continue adhering until firmly attached.

Family

NESTLE PHOTOS IN WIRE SWIRLS

Torrey displays photos, title and journaling in creative, handcrafted wire swirls. Tear patterned vellum (Frances Meyer) and layer over background paper stamped with clear pigment ink (Tsukineko) in a swirled design (Uptown Design). Cut triangles; mount at two corners of background paper. Double mat photos. Print title and journaling; cut to size and tear edges. Follow the instructions below to create these interesting wire photo holders. Nestle photos, title and text block in wire design; mount title and one photo with self-adhesive foam spacers.

Torrey Miller, Westminster, Colorado

Photos, Heidi Finger, Brighton, Colorado

1 Cut three 10" pieces of thin wire for each holder. Twist wires into spirals, leaving 3-4" for stem.

2 Twist three spiraled wires together at ends to create the "stem" of the photo holder.

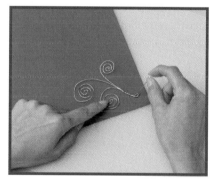

3 To attach to page, position wire on desired place on the page. Use an awl or needle to poke holes on either side of the wire.

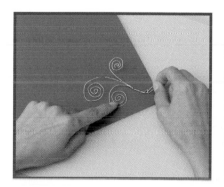

4 Create a "U" out of another piece of wire and poke ends through pre-punched holes.

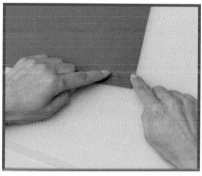

5 On backside of paper, bend "U" back to secure wire. Add more "U" pins if needed to secure wire.

Beads

Round, square, sparkly or opaque, beads are everywhere. String them on fiber or wire to create "necklaces" for your scrapbook page. Glue them in the center of punches or sticker designs for added dimension.

Napa Valley
STRING A BEADED BORDER

Oksanna accents a beautifully layered page with an elegant string of beads and punched hearts. Double-mat patterned paper (Karen Foster Design); slice 3½" wide strips to mount at top and bottom of page. Double mat one photo; mount all photos on page. Print partial title on vellum and solid papers. Diagonally tear vellum; mount at lower right-hand corner. Cut title block; mat on corrugated paper and layer over vellum. Cut large title word with template (C-Thru Ruler); mat largest letter and silhouette cut. String punched hearts (All Night Media) and beads (source unknown); mount horizontally, securing to back of page.

Oksanna Pope, Los Gatos, California

Love for a Lifetime
EMBELLISH PUNCHED SHAPES WITH BEADS

Shannon highlights one of her all-time favorite photos with bead-embellished hearts. Triple-mat enlarged photo. Print title and journaling; cut to size and mat. Silhouette-cut the word "love"; mat and silhouette again. Punch hearts (Marvy) from paper and two-sided adhesive tape (Art Accents). Layer adhesive on hearts before affixing beads (Westrim).

Shannon Taylor, Bristol, Tennessee

Sweet Smile

ADD SPARKLE WITH BEAD CLUSTERS

Valerie combines a variety of embellishments to add sparkle and texture to mother-daughter portraits. Slice strips of vellum and patterned (Mustard Moon) papers; mount horizontally. Mount fiber (Cut-It-Up). Cut two rectangles from solid and patterned papers; mount at upper left and lower right corners. Cut mesh (Avant Card) designs; mount. Mount clusters of beads (Westrim) with crystal lacquer (Sakura Hobby Craft) to form checkerboard design as shown below. Stamp die cut 1" squares (Accu Cut) with title letters (Stampin' Up). Mount on page. Journal with blue pen.

Valerie Barton, Flowood, Mississippi

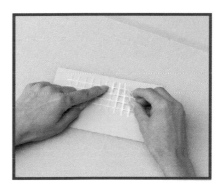

1 Attach Magic Mesh to cardstock. It is self adhesive.

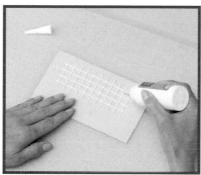

2 Fill squares in Magic Mesh with crystal lacquer.

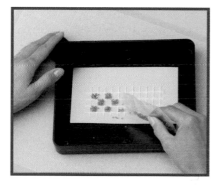

3 Pour beads into crystal-lacquered square and allow to dry. Use tidy tray for neatness.

4 Shake off excess beads into tidy tray. Allow lacquer to dry.

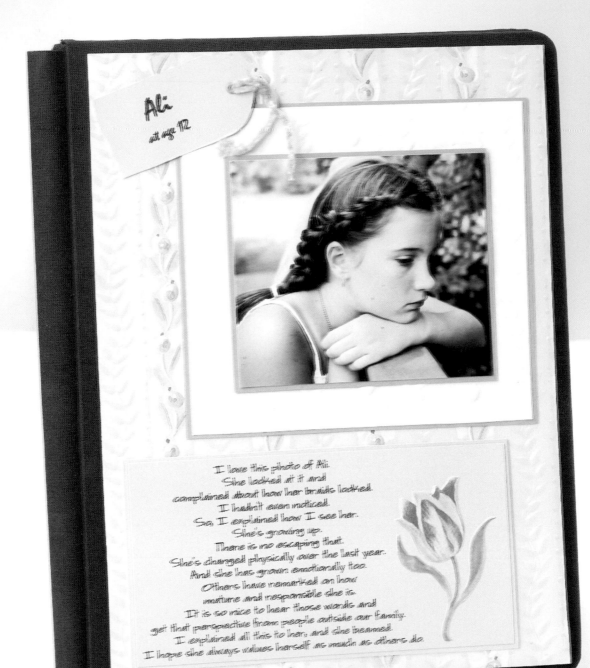

Ali
at age 12

I love this photo of Ali.
She looked at it and
complained about how her braids looked.
I hadn't even noticed.
So, I explained how I see her.
She's growing up.
There is no escaping that.
She's changed physically over the last year.
And she has grown emotionally too.
Others have remarked on how
mature and responsible she is.
It is so nice to hear those words and
get that perspective from people outside our family.
I explained all this to her, and she beamed.
I hope she always values herself as much as others do.

Chapter 5
Journaling

If you could be there in person every time your album was opened, you could recount the story behind each page. However, in most cases this kind of hands-on sharing of information simply isn't possible. Therefore, it is imperative to record your thoughts and feelings in print on your pages so your spreads can speak for themselves. That's why scrapbookers journal.

Through journaling, you'll assure that future generations know who that bright-eyed child in the photograph is, where the photo was taken, when and why. Journaling is your voice, your artistic statement and your interpretation of the world. No two people are exactly alike, nor are two journaling styles the same. Find your style and your voice and your pages will truly reflect your individuality.

What Is a Weed?

STAMP A JOURNALED QUOTE

Greta found the perfect quote to accompany photos of her son exploring a field of dandelions. Single and double mat photos; tear sides of second mat and chalk around edges. Attach flat-top eyelets (Stamp Doctor) at corners of second matting. String fiber (On The Surface) around matting, secure under flat-top eyelets. Tear side border strip on one side; chalk around edges and distress with ink splotches. Stamp quote (Hero Arts). Wrap border with fibers and wire strand adorned with beads and charms. Mount to page with flat-top eyelets.

Greta Hammond, Goshen, Indiana

Cool Quotes

Of all days, the day on which one has not laughed is the one most surely wasted.
Sébastien-Roch Nicolas de Chamfort

Friendship is a single soul dwelling in two bodies.
Aristotle

I'm not afraid of storms, for I have learned how to sail my ship.
Louisa May Alcott

The world is a book, and those who do not travel, read only a page.
Saint Augustine

Shoot for the moon, even if you miss, you'll land amongst the stars.
Les Brown

The longer I live the more beautiful life becomes.
Frank Lloyd Wright

Those who dream by day are cognizant of many things which escape those who dream only by night.
Edgar Allen Poe

Proud to Be an American

ENHANCE PHOTOS WITH SONG-LYRIC JOURNALING

A moving patriotic song sets the perfect tone for Beckie's page. Single and double mat photos on solid and metallic papers. Cut rectangle from gold metallic paper; mount vellum to back of frame. Tear hole from vellum's center; mount photo behind. Print song lyrics on vellum. Slice vellum into strips and layer over photos. Embellish with twisted red and blue fibers (Fibers by the Yard) secured with small gold brads (HyGlo/American Pin). Print title; silhouette cut. Embellish corrugated die-cut star (MPR Associates) with torn paper and eyelet. Dangle flag charm (Zip Clips) with gold embroidery thread (DMC). Mount decorative tag (source unknown) at bottom of right page; frame with eyelets and silver thread (DMC).

Beckie Reaster, Deltona, Florida

There is no more lovely, friendly and charming relationship, communion or
company than a good marriage.
Martin Luther

Some people come into your life only for a moment but leave footprints on your heart
that last forever.
Unknown

Progress involves risks. You can't steal second and keep your foot on first.
Frederick Wilcox

We do not know the true value of our moments until they have undergone the test of memory.
Georges Duhames

Only those who dare to fail can ever achieve greatly.
Robert Francis Kennedy

You never really leave a place you love—You take part of it with you,
leaving part of you behind.
Unknown

Keep your face to the sunshine and you cannot see the shadows.
Helen Keller

Don't cry because it's over—smile because it happened.
Dr. Souss

Simply Beautiful

ENHANCE PHOTOS WITH REFLECTIVE JOURNALING

Jane celebrates her daughter's inner spirit with reflective journaling about who she is, and who she is becoming. Pair an enlarged photo, printed on vellum, with sentimentally journaled thoughts. Offset smaller photo with matted paper square behind upper left-hand corner. Print title and journaling; paper-tear edges before matting on page. Thread buttons (Making Memories) with fibers (On The Surface) before mounting on paper squares.

Jane Rife, Hendersonville, Tennessee

A Man of Style

DOCUMENT A FAMILY MEMBER'S LIFE

A short, concise biography full of fond memories helps Kelly learn about the father-in-law she never met. Mount matted and cropped photos on matted background paper. Adhere sticker border (Creative Imaginations) on solid paper; silhouette cut and layer at left side of page. Adhere sticker letters (Creative Imaginations) on patterned paper (Colorbök). Frame title block with solid paper strips mitered at corners. Chalk edges for dimension; stitch buttons and mount on frame. Print biography onto patterned paper, leaving room for sticker letter. Mat on solid paper; mount to page with gold photo corners. Embellish with fibers EK Success) and stitched buttons.

Kelly Angard, Highlands Ranch, Colorado

Successful Interview Techniques

- Schedule interviews as far ahead as possible to avoid possible scheduling conflicts.
- Brainstorm questions prior to the interview. Ask yourself, "What would I, as an outsider, want to know about this person?"
- Observe your subject's vocal tone, appearance, expressions and gestures. Note them in your writing.
- Ask open-ended questions (rather than yes/no questions) which leave your subject room to expand upon answers.
- Use body language to encourage your subject, including nods and vocal affirmations.
- Take notes during an interview.
- Double-check facts for spellings and dates.

Friends

EXPAND A TITLE INTO JOURNALING

Diana expands her stamped title into an acrostic poem that describes a special friendship. Crumple and iron paper before stamping title (Hero Arts) and printing text on background paper. Add texture to contrasting narrow strip of cardstock by spraying both sides of cardstock with water until very damp. Crumple paper; smooth out and iron without steam until dry. Layer over background paper; mount with flat-top eyelets (Doodlebug Design). Print photo captions on vellum; trim to size and clip (Clipiola) to textured paper. Paper-tear rectangle; mount 3-D sticker (EK Success).

Diana Hudson, Bakersfield, California

Ethan

ILLUSTRATE A PERSONALITY WITH ADJECTIVES

Mary surrounds photos of her son with descriptive words detailing his personality and appearance. Layer solid and patterned (Making Memories) papers for borders and backgrounds. Attach fiber (Lion Brand Yarn) across top of page and border. Mat photos on solid and patterned (Making Memories) papers. Double mat large photo with paper yarn-wrapped (Making Memories) cardstock; mount with self-adhesive foam spacers. Adhere sticker letters (MAMBI) to matted rectangles. Cut rectangle for title; adhere sticker letters (Colorbök), mat and attach buttons (Making Memories).

Mary Faith Roell, Harrison, Ohio

Here's just the right adjective

Use the list below to help spark your imagination.

A ~ athletic, artsy, academic, adventurous, ambitious, active
B ~ bold, bright, beautiful, brainy, brave, busy, boastful, blunt
C ~ creative, cute, cuddly, courageous, confident, carefree
D ~ daring, dreamer, dainty, dramatic, driven, down-to-earth
E ~ energetic, eccentric, excitable, eager-to-please, elegant
F ~ friendly, flirtatious, fun, flamboyant, faithful, full of life
G ~ go-getter, gifted, generous, gentle, gullible, goal-oriented
H ~ happy-go-lucky, humble, hardworking, honest, headstrong
I ~ intelligent, intuitive, impulsive, idealistic, independent
J ~ joker, jovial, joyous, jolly, judgmental, juvenile, jaunty
K ~ kind, keen, kindhearted
L ~ lovely, lucky, lovable, lazy, loyal, liberal, liar
M ~ mysterious, messy, modest, magnetic, mellow, mature

N ~ naughty, neat, nice, naïve, nitpicky, nimble
O ~ outgoing, overachiever, optimistic, open-minded
P ~ practical, perfectionist, popular, passionate, polite, picky
Q ~ quiet, quick, quirky, quixotic, quarrelsome
R ~ responsible, romantic, rowdy, reliable, religious, risk-taker
S ~ shy, smart, stubborn, sensitive, spiritual, superstitious
T ~ talkative, trustworthy, thoughtful, talented, trusting
U ~ unique, unconventional, unpredictable, unruly, upbeat
V ~ vibrant, vain, vivacious, vulnerable, visionary, vindictive
W ~ worldly, well-liked, willful, wise beyond his/her years
X ~ x-pert, x-tremist, xenophobic
Y ~ youthful, young-for-his/her-age, yappy
Z ~ zany, zestful, zealous, zingy, zippy

Take the Christmas Picture!

CAPTURE HIDDEN THOUGHTS

Although Peggy loves getting a perfect holiday portrait of her girls, the process requires lots of patience, a sense of humor, and a creative mind! Mount photos on red patterned paper (Crafter's Workshop). Tear top of matting, attach eyelet (Prym-Dritz) and fibers (Quilter's Resource Inc.). Attach fibers horizontally along page bottom, leaving space for captions. Print captions onto patterned paper (Crafter's Workshop). Trim to size and detail around edges with black pen. Print title words; cut to size and mat. Print word "trying" on velvet paper; silhouette-cut and mount on vellum. Attach eyelets at top; bend wire adorned with beads (JewelCraft) to resemble hanger. Attach to page with small brad (Impress Rubber Stamps).

Peggy Kangas, Pepperell, Massachusetts

Quick Tip: Find great quotes in songs and poems, quote-of-the-day calendars, Web sites, quote books (A favorite: "The 2,548 Best Things Anybody Ever Said" by Robert Byrne), interviews with experts, political and inspirational speeches, posters and greeting cards.

I Am Growing

NARRATE JOURNALED BORDERS

Stacy gives her pup a voice with first-person journaling narrating his first year of life. Slice two strips of colored paper, one ¼" larger than the other; layer at outer edges of solid paper. Lightly stamp border with paw prints (Close To My Heart) and background paper with dog-related images (Close To My Heart) using Versa Mark ink (Tsukineko). Double mat small photos. Lightly stamp blue cardstock with bones (Close To My Heart); mat large photo with stamped cardstock. Slice thin strips of dark blue paper; mount diagonally over opposite corners of matted photo. Cut title letters with template (Scrap Pagerz) from blue stamped cardstock. Mat and silhouette cut. Print journaling list on vellum; mount.

Stacy MacLaren, Tucson, Arizona

Point of View

LET PERSPECTIVE JOURNALING DO THE TALKING

Kelli gives each subject in her photo a voice detailing what it was like growing up together. Double mat photo; use two colors of paper for first matting. Slice strips of complementary-colored paper; mount together for a small, color-blocked title border. Punch title letters (Family Treasures) and mount. Print journaling. Cut to size, mat and mount. Mount metal alphabet brads (Making Memories) to matting.

Kelli Noto, Centennial, Colorado

What Not to Do in Jamaica

JOURNAL THE UNUSUAL

Holly created a unique way to journal about honeymoon photos with a comic list of memories. Color block a background with monochromatic shades of brown by layering rectangles of various dimensions. Mat photos. Craft journal tags by cutting computer-printed journaling to size and laminate. Mount large eyelets (Prym-Dritz) and tie fibers (source unknown). Cut title letters from templates (C-Thru Ruler and Scrap Pagerz); detail with black pen on small letters. Mat large letters and silhouette cut.

Holly Van Dyne, Mansfield, Ohio

Top 10 Reasons

JOURNAL A LIST OF LOVE

Holle chronicles a little girl's love for her grandma with a clever "top 10" list. Double mat photos; tear right side of second mat; mount on page as a left-side border over patterned background paper (Frances Meyer). Print journal list; tear edges and crumple. Mat on solid paper; tear across top. Mat leaf sticker (Karen Foster Design); mount on journal matting. Adhere leaf stickers to left side border.

Holle Wiktorek, Fayetteville, North Carolina

Christmas Eve Checklist

DETAIL HOLIDAY TRADITIONS

Dee designed a clever checklist detailing her family's Christmas Eve traditions. Layer torn solid and patterned (Doodlebug Designs) paper over patterned (Paper Fever) and solid background papers. Triple mat photo; tear edges of second matting. Attach matted photo to page with eyelets (Stamp Studio) Print checklist and title text. Cut to size; outline with black pen. Cut or punch 1" squares; mat and adhere to page with self-adhesive foam spacers. Cut title letters and check marks from template (Provo Craft). Mat title letters, silhouette and add outlines with black pen. Mount check marks onto matted squares. Handcut tag at page bottom; mat and attach eyelet and fiber (DMC).

Dee Gallimore-Perry,
Griswold, Connecticut

Creative Things to Put in a List

- Best/Worst Dates Ever
- Life Lessons I Have Learned
- Songs That Make Me Cry
- Coolest Family Traditions
- Best Movies Ever Made
- Favorite Family Memories

- Significant Career Highlights
- Best Gifts Ever Received
- Wildest Thing I Ever Did
- Most Respected People and Why
- Ickiest Foods or Ickiest Fashions
- What I MUST Remember to Tell My Grandchildren Someday

100 Percent Boy

Torrey came up with the perfect recipe for a page that screams "100 Percent Boy!" Tear solid-colored paper strip; mount on background paper. Double mat photo; partially layer over torn paper strip. Mount die-cut title letters (Ellison/Provo Craft); detail with black pen. Layer die-cut ladybugs (Ellison/Provo Craft); mount on page. Create recipe card on computer and print journaling.

Torrey Miller, Westminster, Colorado

Della Osborne

CELEBRATE SOMEONE'S LIFE WITH A TIMELINE

In Jodi's heritage, nobody goes unnoticed! Mount photo five times. Use embroidery floss (DMC) to create a border around the third mat by blanket stitching into punched wholes. Across patterned paper (Anna Griffin), draw and stitch timeline. Attach timeline journaling blocks. Mount patterned paper on darker colored cardstock.

Jodi Amidei, Memory Makers

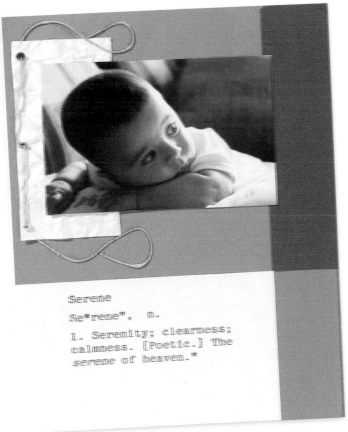

Serene

GIVE DEFINITION TO PHOTO SUBJECT

Desiree clearly defines a serene moment with dictionary journaling. Color block background with natural shades of cardstock. Print text on ivory cardstock before mounting on page. Add texture to photo matting by crumpling ivory cardstock; flatten and add definition with chalk. Attach eyelets; weave hemp cord through eyelets and mount on page.

Desiree McClellan, Decatur, Alabama

Priceless

CREATE A JOURNALING TAG

Jodi documents the story behind a found treasure on a fiber-tied tag. Mat patterned paper (Scrap Ease); mount large rectangle of solid paper at center. Mount fiber (EK Success) horizontally over solid paper; secure behind page. Single and double mat photos; mount center photo with self-adhesive foam spacers for dimension. Print title and journaling onto solid paper; cut to size and mount on tag. Tie fibers (EK Success) onto tag.

Jodi Amidei, Memory Makers

35 Uses for Your Golden Retriever

PUT TOGETHER A THEMED ALBUM

Katie created a lighthearted, pet-themed album for her husband that became his favorite holiday gift! Make a simple themed album by printing consistent borders and text. Use your computer to keep the letters tidy. Mat photos; mount on pages.

Katie Nelson, Murray, Utah

35 Uses
for
Your
Golden
Retriever

Bed Warmer

Safety Inspector on
all stuffed animals

Great Interview Questions

PAST

Where were you born?

What is your first memory?

What did you do for fun as a child?

What lessons did you learn "the hard way"?

What did you get away with that your parents never knew about?

PRESENT

Who are the most important people in your life and why?

What is a typical day like for you?

What are your greatest accomplishments? Failures?

What are your hobbies?

What is your biggest dream?

Describe yourself using only three adjectives.

What are your best qualities? Worst?

FUTURE

What do you want to change (or stay the same) in your life?

What is the one dream you fear you'll never be able to fulfill?

What challenges do you anticipate in the future?

If you could have one wish, what would it be?

What's one thing you know now that you wish you knew then?

Quick Tip: During an interview don't forget to ask your subject if she has any old photos. She may let you make copies to use in your scrapbook. Old photos are also great for sparking memories.

Once Upon a Time

WRITE A PERSONALIZED FAIRY TALE

Kelly wrote a modern-day fairy tale about a few favorite princesses who teach lessons of love and friendship. Print story on vellum, leaving room for illuminated letter. Cut to size; detail with black pen around edges. Cut window for photo in vellum with craft knife. Mount over photo and matted background paper (Frances Meyer) with flower eyelets (Making Memories) at corners. Silhouette-cut large letter printed from computer; mat on glittery paper (Paper Adventures). Mount flat-backed jewels (Magic Scraps) on letter and page. Double and triple mat photos.

Kelly Angard, Highlands Ranch, Colorado

Gallery

More beautiful quick & easy scrapbook pages for inspiration.

Slip Sliding Away

DRAW ATTENTION TO PHOTOS

Brandi's simple layout keeps her photos as the focal point of the page. Cut large square of patterned paper (Scrappin' Dreams); layer over patterned background paper (Magenta). Mount cropped photos. Print title and journaling onto vellum; mat on yellow patterned paper strip and square. Tie buttons (Making Memories) with embroidery thread; mount on page.

Brandi Ginn, Lafayette, Colorado

Photos, Joann Brennan, Centennial, Colorado

Blossoms

BRING PHOTO IMAGES TO LIFE

Large flower die cuts adorn Torrey's colorful page of blossoms. Cut large circles from patterned papers (Karen Foster Design, Paper Adventures); layer on matted patterned paper (Doodlebug Design). Mat photos; layer over circles as shown. Die cut title letters and flowers (Accu Cut). Mount on page; give dimension to flowers by mounting one with self-adhesive foam spacers. Print journaling; cut to size and mount.

Torrey Miller, Westminster, Colorado

Summer Girls

HAVE THE COLOR SET THE MOOD

Soft pastel-colored, patterned papers set the tone for a sweet summer moment between friends. Mat photo on patterned paper (Karen Foster Design). Tear bottom edge of matting; mount on patterned background paper (Making Memories). Print title and journaling onto vellum. Cut to size and layer over torn patterned paper (Karen Foster Design). Mount title to page with eyelets (Doodlebug Design).

Brandi Ginn, Lafayette, Colorado
Photos, Lori White, Visalia, California

Frye Cove Park

HIGHLIGHT EYE-CATCHING BACKGROUND

Andrea layers colored vellum on her color-blocked background for a simple and striking effect. Print title and journaling onto background paper. Print selected words on blue paper, leaving space to tear around edges. Mount directly over previously printed word. Cut rectangles of varying dimensions from blue and green vellum; layer on page as shown. Mount photo.

Andrea Hautala, Olympia, Washington

Brothers

CALL ATTENTION TO A SPECIAL PICTURE

Donna "hangs" a favorite photo of her sons on a page framed with unevenly cut paper strips. Mat photo; cut to size and tear all sides of matting. Punch small holes through matted photo. Tie embroidery thread with beads (Magic Scraps) to photo; hang from brad (Hyglo/American Pin) attached to page. Print title and journaling; cut to size and tear edges. Punch small holes in title/text block; secure to page with embroidery thread and brads.

Donna Goodman, Seville, Florida

Cars

INCORPORATE STICKERS INTO TITLE

Jennifer highlights her love of stickers by using a large car sticker in her title. Double mat photo. Mount over triple-matted patterned paper (Paper Patch). Print text; cut to size and mat. Cut title letters from template (Scrap Pagerz); mat and silhouette. Adhere car stickers (Provo Craft) in title and page bottom.

Jennifer Blackham, West Jordan, Utah

Catch the Wave

TEAR A SPECIAL DESIGN

Oksanna crafted an enormous swooping wave from torn pieces of colored vellum. Tear strips of clear, blue and silver vellum in various widths and lengths; layer on page in desired shape over patterned background paper (Design Originals). Highlight wave with clear dimensional paint (Duncan). Single, double and triple mat cropped photos. Cut title letters from template (EZ2Cut); add punched fishes (EK Success) on letters.

Oksanna Pope, Los Gatos, California

Park

SHOWCASE METAL EMBELLISHMENTS

Greta showcases her keen eye for simplistic detail with a black-and-white photo layout. Mat solid, torn paper with lightly chalked edges. Slice 1" strip; mat on top and bottom of both pages. Single mat photos. "Hang" one photo with linked jump rings (source unknown). Attach to matted strip with flat-top eyelets (Stamp Doctor). Mount metal letters (Making Memories) with self-adhesive foam spacers. Link letters with artist's wire (Artistic Wire); hang. Stamp date (Hero Arts); frame with metal tag (Making Memories) and attach with eyelets (Making Memories). Print journaling; cut to size and layer over solid paper square. Double mat three photos; add flat-top eyelets to left side of one and paper tear another. For bottom left photo, cut second mat 1½" longer on left. Fold over photo; attach eyelets over small punched squares.

Greta Hammond, Goshen, Indiana

Time

USE EVERYDAY SUPPLIES TO CREATE BORDER

Andrea borders the top of her page with layered embellishments torn from a greeting card. Layer patterned paper (C-Thru Ruler) over solid paper for background. Mount sheer ribbon (Offray) across top of page; secure ends around back of page. Mount flower embellishments torn from greeting card. Double mat photo; mount. Print journaling two times from computer onto two colors of solid paper. Cut one to size for journal block; ink around edges and center to soften stark white color. Highlight text by cutting out specific words on alternate-colored paper and mounting over previously printed word.

Andrea Hautala, Olympia, Washington

Dr. Seuss

PRESERVE A PRICELESS MEMORY WITH A QUOTE

Andrea captures her daughter's personality with a reflective poem adorned with creative paper clips. Print poem, separating lines so each can be cut apart. Cut to size; detail around edges with black pen. Mat two text blocks with patterned paper (Provo Craft); slice corrugated paper strips and mount horizontally at top and bottom of page. Attach swirled paper clips (Target) to text blocks; mount. Mat photo and mount.

Andrea Hunsella, Olympia, Washington

Pay No Mind

CREATE A DELICATE BORDER

Torn paper provides a soft, textured border for a meaningful poem and the simple embellishments on Cindy's page. Mat solid paper. Print poem on yellow cardstock; tear one side and layer over solid-colored paper at outer edges. Mat photos; mount. Handcut hearts; tear around edges. Mount on page and on matted paper rectangles with eyelets (Stamp Studio). Tie fibers (Fibers by the Yard) together; secure ends under matted paper rectangles.

Cindy Sherman, Columbia, Tennessee

Royce

GIVE "VOICE" TO A UNIQUE PERSONALITY

Oksanna brings her son's personality to life with a number of nicknames creatively displayed on the page. Print journaling on solid-colored paper. Cut to size; trim with decorative scissors. Detail journal block with leaf stickers (Provo Craft) and hand-drawn design with black pen. Layer over patterned paper (Anna Griffin) rectangle. Cut title letters using a template (EZ2Cut); add punched swirls (All Night Media). Mat photo on patterned paper; slice and mount on both pages.

Oksanna Pope, Los Gatos, California

Curiosity

LET LAYOUT DEFINE MOOD

Emily captures the natural curiosity of her toddler with an interesting, rustic layout. Crop photos; mount on patterned paper (Scrap Ease). Cut mat into quarters, crumple and loosely attach pieces together with cotton thread (Making Memories) wrapped around small brads (Creative Impressions). Mat large photo on distressed photo mat. Print title and journaling on solid paper. Cut to size and mount.

Emily Marjamaa, Fort Collins, Colorado

Dreaming of Lazy Days

CREATE A SEASONAL FEEL

Amy layers soft textures in warm colors inspired by her favorite season of the year. Tear solid-colored paper borders; gently curl torn edges with fingers. Tear mulberry paper into geometric shapes; assemble into sun as shown. Single and double mat photos on torn mulberry and solid papers; curl edges in same fashion as borders. Print quote and journaling onto solid-colored paper. Handcut into tag shape; punch hole at top and tear at bottom. Tie raffia to tags. Stamp title letters (Plaid Enterprises) to paper strips; cut to size and mount.

Amy Barnett-Arthur
Liberty Township, Ohio

Royce

LET THE PHOTO SAY IT ALL

Oksanna focuses in on a few favorite details with partial images of her son displayed in the page's title. Layer patterned paper (Provo Craft) square over solid background paper. Print journaling on solid-colored paper; detail with hand-drawn design around edges with black pen before mounting. Cut photo title letters from template (C-Thru Ruler); mat and silhouette cut. Stamp dragonfly (All Night Media); add gold hand-drawn design around page with metallic dimensional paint (Duncan) and gold gel pen.

Oksanna Pope, Los Gatos, California

Glossary of scrapbook terms and techniques

Acid-Free

Look for scrapbook products—particularly pages, paper, adhesives and inks—that are free from harmful acids that can eat away at the emulsion of your photos. Harmful acids can occur in the manufacturing process. Check labels for "acid-free" and "photo-safe."

Archival Quality

A nontechnical term suggesting that a substance is chemically stable, durable and permanent.

Border

The upper, lower and side edges or margins of a scrapbook page. Sometimes refers to a border design that is handmade or manufactured and attached to a page. See pages 58-67.

Chronological

Arranged in order of time occurrence as it pertains to the sorting, organizing and/or placement of photos and memorabilia throughout your album.

Design

A visual compostion or pattern of photos, journaling and accessories that ultimately becomes a finished scrapbook page. See pages 14-25.

Embellishments

Page accents you can make or buy. Can include stickers, die cuts, stamped images, punch art, beads, buttons, rhinestones, sequins, pens, chalks, inkpads, charms, wire, ribbon, embroidery floss, thread and much more. See pages 74-97.

Journaling

Refers to handwritten, handmade or computer-generated text that provides pertinent details about what is taking place in photographs. See pages 98-113.

Layout

To put or spread photos and memorabilia in readiness for scrapbooking or a sketch of a scrapbook page design. See pages 14-25.

Lignin-Free

Paper and paper products that are void of the material (sap) that holds wood fibers together as a tree grows. Most paper is lignin-free except for newsprint, which yellows and becomes brittle with age. Check product labels to be on the safe side.

Matting

The act of attaching paper, generally cropped in the shape of a photo, behind the photo to separate it from the scrapbook page's background paper. See pages 68-73.

Memorabilia

Mementos and souvenirs saved from travel, school and life's special events—things that are worthy of remembrance.

Page Protectors

Plastic sleeves or pockets that encase finished scrapbook pages for protection. Use only PVC-free protectors.

Photo-Safe

A term used by companies to indicate they feel their products are safe to use with photos in a scrapbook album.

Preservation

The act of stabilizing an item from deterioration by using the proper methods and materials manufactured to maintain the conditions and longevity of the item.

PVC or polyvinyl chloride

A plastic that should not be used in a scrapbook, it emits gases, which interact with and cause damage to photos. Use only PVC-free plastic page protectors and memorabilia keepers. Safe plastics include polypropylene, polyethylene, and polyester or Mylar.

Title

A general or descriptive headline put on a scrapbook page that sums up its overall theme. See pages 50-57.

Daniel, page 6

DOCUMENT A SPECIAL VACATION

Thanks to this memorable layout, Michele will always treasure memories of her family's summer trip to Alaska. Diagonally tear middle from sheet of patterned paper (Karen Foster Design). Place mesh (Avant Card) mounted on brown cardstock inside gap. Mount photos on white cardstock; place on strips of corrugated dark green cardstock. Adhere pictures. Repeat same technique as seen on the bacground to make the tag (DMD). Place sticker letters (Mrs. Grossman's) on shapes. Add leather strap (Crafter's Workshop) and journaling.

Jodi Amidei, Memory Makers

Photos, Michele Gerbrandt

Summer Fruits, page 14

CAPTURE THE ESSENSE OF A SEASON

Jenna's simple, pastel layout perfectly mirrors the carefree feeling of summer. Cut mats out of two different colors of vellum; chalk edges. Mount double-matted photo on chalked vellum pieces. Journal on vellum; chalk; adhere in place with pear stickers (EK Success). Cut letters using lettering templates (Scrap Pagerz); chalk edges before adhering.

Jenna Beegle, Woodstock, Georgia

Sand, page 32

USE CORRESPONDING COLORS TO ACCENT A THEME

Jodi captured the beauty of her daughter's sand dune experience with a layout that looks as though it were carved right out of sand! Triple mount photo on cream, then crumpled brown, then cream cardstocks. Place pop-dots between two outermost layers of cardstock. Tear two different colors of lighter brown cardstock and mount on third, darker brown color. Hand-letter two titles; tear edges; accent with chalk. Adhere eyelet letters (Making Memories) for third title. Print journaling on vellum. Using chalk, highlight the word "sand" on backside of vellum. Attach with eyelets.

Jodi Amidei, Memory Makers

Tom, page 48

SHOWCASE MATCHING TITLES, BORDERS AND MATTING

Jodi reminisces on her husband's finer qualities with a sentimental, co-ordinating layout. Mat photos on light green cardstock, leaving room for wire embellishments. Add wire embellishments; re-mat in dark green. Cut thin paper strips and squares for title. Using a stencil (EK Success), dab ink from a stamp ink pad (Stampin' Up) through to spell name; add wire embellishments. Stamp leaf image over homemade tag; mat in dark green. Print vellum journaling; adhere over tag with eyelets (Impress Rubber Stamps).

Jodi Amidei, Memory Makers

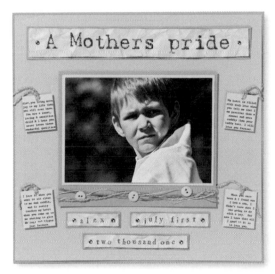

A Mother's Pride, page 74

LET THE TAGS DO THE TALKING

Trudy highlights a few of the things she loves most about her son by printing them on individual, homemade tags. Mount enlarged photo; adorn with fibers and buttons along bottom edge (Magic Scraps; Making Memories; On The Surface). Pop out picture with pop dots. Print journaling and cut into small square tags. Print titles and word blocks; crumple. Adhere to page with brads.

Trudy Sigurdson, Victoria, BC, Canada

Ali, page 98

JOURNAL YOUR INNERMOST THOUGHTS

Lisa shares her feelings about watching her daughter grow up in this truly personal poem. Triple mat photo on sage and cream-embossed papers (K & Company). Create tag (Ellison/Provo Craft); tear edges and add fibers. Print journaling; mount on light pink cardstock. Add flower sticker (K & Company).

Lisa Simon, Roanoke, Virginia

Professional Photographers

Keepsake Photography
254 Park Ave. West
Mansfield, OH 44903   419-522-8363

Joann Brennan
Centennial, Colorado

Contributing Memory Makers Masters

Valerie Barton, Brandi Ginn, Diana Hudson, Torrey Miller, Kelli Noto, Heidi Schueller, Trudy Sigurdson, Holle Wiktorek

Sources

The following companies manufacture products featured in this book. Please check your local retailers to find these materials. We have made every attempt to properly credit the items mentioned in this book. We apologize to any company that we have listed incorrectly or the sources were unknown.

3L Corp.
800-828-3130 3lcorp.com

Accu-Cut®
800-288-1670 accucut.com
(wholesale only)

All My Memories
888-553-1998 allmymemories.com

All Night Media®
800-782-6733

American Tag Company
800-223-3956

American Tombow, Inc.
800-835-3232 tombowusa.com

Anna Griffin, Inc.
888-817-8170 annagriffin.com
(wholesale only)

Art Accents, Inc.
360-733-898
artaccents.net

Artistic Wire, Ltd.™
630-530-7567
artisticwire.com

Autumn Leaves
800-588-6707
(wholesale only)

Avant Card avantcard.com.au

Avery Dennison Corporation
310-937-4868

Bazzill Basics Paper
480-558-8557 bazzillbasics.com
(wholesale only)

Beadery®, The
401-539-2432

Blumenthal Lansing Co.
563-538-4211

Carolee's Creations®
435-563-1100 carolees.com
(wholesale only)

Centis
888-236-8476 centis.com

Charming Pages
888-889-5060
charmingpages.com (wholesale only)

Close To My Heart®
888-655-6552 closetomyheart.com

Clipiola
No contact info. available

Club Scrap™
888-634-9100 clubscrap.com

Colorbök™
800-366-4660 colorbok.com
(wholesale only)

Colors By Design
800-832-8436 colorsbydesign.com

Crafter's Workshop, The
877-CRAFTER thecraftersworkshop.com

Craf-T Products
507-235-3996

Crafts, Etc., Ltd.
800-888-0321 craftsetc.com

Creative Imaginations
800-942-6487 cigift.com
(wholesale only)

Creative Impressions
719-577-4858

Creative Memories®
800-468-9335 creative-memories.com

C-Thru® Ruler Company, The
800-243-8419 cthruruler.com
(wholesale only)

Cut-It-Up™
cut-it-up.com

Darice, Inc.
800-321-1494 darice.com

DayCo Ltd.
877-595-8160 daycodiecuts.com

Debbie Mumm®
888-819-2923

Deluxe Cuts™
480-497-9005 deluxecuts.com

DeNami Design Rubber Stamps
253-437-1626

Design Originals
800-877-7820 d-originals.com

Designs for the Needle
no contact information available

DieCuts With a View™
877-221-6107

DL Designs
no contact info. available

DMC Corp.
dmc–usa.com

DMD Industries, Inc.
800-805-9890 dmdind.com
(wholesale only)

Doodlebug Design Inc.™
801-966-9962

Duncan Enterprises
559-294-3282 duncan-enterprises.com
(wholesale only)

EarthGoods™
800-469-HEMP earthgds.com

EK Success™ Ltd.
800-524-1349 eksuccess.com
(wholesale only)

Ellison® Craft and Design
800-253-2238 ellison.com

Emagination Crafts, Inc.
630-833-9521 emaginationcrafts.com
(wholesale only)

Eyelet Factory™, The
801-582-3606 eyeletfactory.com
(wholesale only)

EZ2Cut Templates
260-489-9212 ez2cut.com

Family Treasures, Inc.®
familytreasures.com

Faux Memories
813-269-7946 fauxmemories.com

Fibers by the Yard
fibersbytheyard.com

Fiskars, Inc.
715-842-2091 fiskars.com
(wholesale only)

Frances Meyer, Inc.®
800-372-6237 francesmeyer.com

Graphic Products Corporation
800-323-1660

Halcraft USA, Inc.
212-376-1580

Hasbro
hasbro.com

Hero Arts® Rubber Stamps, Inc.
800-822-4376 heroarts.com
(wholesale only)

Hillcreek Designs
619-562-5799 hillcreekdesigns.com

Hirschberg Schutz & Co., Inc.
800-221-8640

Hyglo®/American Pin
800-821-7125 american-pin.com
(wholesale only)

Impress Rubber Stamps
206-901-9101
impressrubberstamps.com

Jennifer Collection
no contact information available

Jest Charming
702-564-5101 jestcharming.com
(wholesale only)

Jesse James & Co., Inc.
610-435-0201 jessejamesbutton.com

JewelCraft, LLC
201-223-0804 jewelcraft.biz

Judi Kins
310-515-1115

Just Another Button Company
618-667-8531 (wholesale only)

K & Co.
888-244-2083 kandcompany.com
(wholesale only)

Karen Foster Design
801-451-9779

Keeping Memories Alive™
800-419-4949 scrapbooks.com

Lion Brand Yarn Company
lionbrand.com

Magenta Rubber Stamps
800-565-5254 magentarubberstamps.com
(wholesale only)

Magic Scraps™
972-385-1838 magicscraps.com

Making Memories
800-286-5263 makingmemories.com

Marvy® Uchida
800-541-5877 uchida.com
(wholesale only)

McGill, Inc.
800-982-9884 mgillinc.com

Me & My Big Ideas
949-589-4607 meandmybigideas.com
(wholesale only)

Memory Crafts
memorycrafts.com

Mercer Motifs, Inc. (ChYOPS)
801-205-3268

Microsoft
microsoft.com

MPR Associates, Inc.
336-861-6343

Mrs. Grossman's Paper Co.
800-429-4549 mrsgrossmans.com
(wholesale only)

Mustard Moon™ Paper
408-229-8542 mustardmoon.com

Offray & Son, Inc.
offray.com

Okie-Dokie Press, The
801-298-1028

On The Fringe
onthefringe.net

On The Surface
847-675-2520

Paper Adventures®
800-727-0699 paperadventures.com
(wholesale only)

Paper Fever Inc.
801-412-0495

Paper House Productions
800-255-7316

Paper Loft, The
866-254-1961 paperloft.com

Paper Magic Group, The
no contact info. available

Paper Patch®, The
801-253-3018 paperpatch.com
(wholesale only)

Pebbles in my Pocket
pebblesinmypocket.com

Pioneer Photo Albums, Inc.
800-366-3686 pioneerphotoalbums.com

Plaid Enterprises, Inc.
800-842-4197 plaidonline.com

Provo Craft®
888-577-3545 provocraft.com
(wholesale only)

Prym-Dritz Corporation
www.dritz.com

PSX Design™
800-782-6748 psxdesign.com

Punch Bunch, The
254-791-4209 thepunchbunch.com

Quilter's Resource, Inc.
800-676-6543 quiltersresource.com

Rocky Mtn. Scrapbook Co.
801-785-9695 rmscrapbook.com

Rubba Dub Dub Artist's Stamps
707-748-0929
artsanctum.com/RubbaDubDubHome.html

Rubber Stamps of America
800-553-5031

Sakura Hobby Craft
10-212-7878 sakuracraft.com

Sakura of America
800-776-6257 sakuraofamerica.com

Sandylion Sticker Designs
800-387-4215 sandylion.com
(wholesale only)

Scrapbook Sally
435-645-0696 scrapbooksally.com

Scrapbook Wizard™, The
801-947-0019 scrapbookwizard.com

Scrappin' Dreams
417-831-1882 scrappindreams.com

Scrap-Ease®
800-642-6762 e-craftshop.com
(wholesale only)

Scrap-in-a-Snap™
866-462-7627
scrapinasnap.,com

ScrapPagerz
ScrapPagerz.com

SEI, Inc.
800-333-3279 shopsei.com

Stamp Doctor, The
stampdoctor.com

Stamp Studio
208-288-0300

Stampin' Up!®
800-782-6787 stampinup.com

Stickopotamus
888-270-4443 stickopotamus.com

Target
target.com

Treehouse Designs
877-372-1109

Tsukineko® Inc.
800-769-6633 tsukineko.com

Un-du® Products, Inc.
888-289-8638 un-du.com

Uptown Design Company™
800-888-3212 uptowndesign.com

U.S. Shell, Inc.
956-943-1709 usshell.com

Xyron Inc.
800-793-3523 xyron.com

Westrim® Crafts
800-727-2727 westrimcrafts.com

Zip Clips
no contact info. available

Index

B

Backgrounds 32-47

Beads...96-97

Borders 58-67

C

Chalk Embellishing....................................82-83

Color Blocking 40-47

Color Psychology....................................28-29

Color Selection 26-27

Cool Quotes 100-101

Creative Things to Put in a List 109

Creative Titles With Creative Materials 53

Credits and Sources 124-127

D

Dress Up Punches 85

E

Embellishments...74-97

F

Fiber Embellishing 91-93

Fiber Embellishments..93

G

Gallery...114-122

Getting Started 8-13

Glossary of Scrapbook Terms and Techniques 123

Great Interview Questions....................................112

H

Here's Just the Right Adjective 105

I

Introduction 7

J

Journaling,...98-113

L

Layout and Design 15-31

M

Mats 68-73

P

Paper-Torn Embellishing.....................................78-79

Pre-Made Embellishments 76-77

Pre-Made Product 34-39

Punch and Die-Cut Embellishing 84-85

S

Six Ways to Adorn Your Mat...............................73

Six Ways to Use a Stencil 55

Sorting Photos By Theme 9

Sorting Photos Chronologically 8

Stamp Embellishing 86-89

Sticker Borders..63

Sticker Embellishing 80-81

Successful Interview Techniques, ...103

Supplies Shopping Checklist 13

T

Tag Embellishing 90

Templates 16-31

Titles 50-57

Titles, Borders & Mats 48-73

Tools 10

Top Timesaving Tools 11-12

W

Wire Embellishing..94-95